Nathaniel Ingersoll Bowditch, George Edward Ellis

Extracts from a History of the Massachusetts general Hospital

1810-1851

Nathaniel Ingersoll Bowditch, George Edward Ellis

Extracts from a History of the Massachusetts general Hospital
1810-1851

ISBN/EAN: 9783337163419

Printed in Europe, USA, Canada, Australia, Japan

Cover: Foto ©ninafisch / pixelio.de

More available books at **www.hansebooks.com**

EXTRACTS

FROM A

HISTORY

OF THE

MASSACHUSETTS GENERAL HOSPITAL

1810 – 1851

Nathaniel I. Bowditch

WITH A

CONTINUATION

1851–1872

Dr. George E. Ellis

PRIVATELY PRINTED

PREFACE.

THESE extracts have been made for the purpose of presenting in a succinct form the most important events connected with the origin and growth of the Massachusetts General Hospital, and the development and use of the administrative powers of its officers. They are now published, with an index, in the belief that they will be of interest and value to my co-members of the Board of Trustees; and to all other persons who have a professional or a philanthropic regard for the institution.

FRANCIS BLAKE.

FEBRUARY, 1899.

HISTORY

OF THE

MASSACHUSETTS GENERAL HOSPITAL.

EXTRACTS.

At the beginning of the present century, Massachusetts had no Hospital or Insane Asylum, though such institutions had been for many years established in the States of New York and Pennsylvania. There were various indications, however, that the want of such establishments was beginning to be felt in our community. Thomas Boylston, Esq., by will dated Nov. 12, 1798, proved in 1800, made the town of Boston his residuary devisee in trust, among other objects, to erect a small-pox hospital and a lunatic hospital. The testator was, unfortunately, a member of the firm of Lane, Frazier and Company, of London, which became insolvent. Hon. William Phillips, by a codicil dated April 18, 1797, proved in 1804, bequeathed the sum of five thousand dollars to the town of Boston for this object.

August 20, 1810. A circular letter was issued by Drs. James Jackson and John C. Warren inviting subscriptions "for a hospital for the reception of lunatics and other sick persons." This letter may be regarded as the corner-stone of our institution: It contains a perspicuous statement of the advantages which a hospital would extend to all classes of society, and closes as follows: —

"Hospitals and infirmaries are found in all the Christian cities of the Old World; and our large cities in the Middle States have institutions of this sort, which do great honour to the liberality and benevolence of their founders. We flatter ourselves that in this respect, as in all others, Boston may ere long assert her claim to equal praise."

February 25, 1811. Charter obtained from the Legislature. It incorporates James Bowdoin and fifty-five others of the most distinguished inhabitants of the various towns of the Commonwealth, by the name of the Massachusetts General Hospital. The Governor, Lieutenant-Governor, President of the Senate, Speaker of the House, and the Chaplains of both Houses, are constituted a board of Visitors. The institution is placed under the care of twelve Trustees, of whom four are chosen by the board of Visitors. A grant was made of the Province-house Estate, so called, with authority to sell the same and use the proceeds at pleasure, provided that within five years an additional sum of one hundred thousand dollars should be obtained by private subscriptions and donations.

A further term of five years was allowed by an Act of June 14, 1813.

By a resolve passed February 13, 1816, authority was finally granted for sale of the Province House, on the sole condition of giving bond to pay the proceeds of sale into the State Treasury, unless, within one year from such sale, said additional sum of one hundred thousand dollars should be obtained. On April 1, 1817, the Hospital leased this estate to David Greenough, Esq., for ninety-nine years, at an annual rent of two thousand dollars, or an outright sum of thirty-three thousand dollars, at his option; and, on October 1, 1824, he elected to pay this latter sum. The reversion of the estate (to come into possession in A. D. 1916) still remains in the Hospital.

The Province-house Estate, thus liberally given by the Commonwealth, embraced a tract of land measuring eighty-six feet six inches on Washington, formerly Marlborough Street, and extended back two hundred and sixty-seven feet to Governor's Alley or Province Street, where it measured in width seventy-six feet, being about half an acre of land. Stores have now been erected in front on Washington Street; and a block of brick houses, on the northerly side of Province-house Court, stand on the back part of the estate. Its present value is small [assessed for $600,000, 1898]. But the Corporation will live forever; and it is to be hoped that no future Board of Trustees will alienate this, the first donation made to the institution. Rather let it remain to the latest times an enduring monument of the liberality of the Commonwealth, as in times past it was the representative of its official dignity. And, in acknowledgment of this splendid gift, and of the many subsequent benefits derived from the same source, may our institution always preserve unchanged its corporate name of the *Massachusetts* General Hospital!

April 23, 1811. The first meeting of the Corporation was held. The Corporation was organized by [the choice of] a President and Vice-President, Treasurer and Secretary; the Secretary being, *ex officio*, Secretary of the Board of Trustees.

July 5, 1811. By-laws adopted. The thanks of the Corporation were presented to Josiah Loring for the gift of an elegant record-book. [Still used, 1899.]

February 2, 1813. Trustees first chosen. At first, the President always attended the meetings of Trustees, and presided; but, since 1818, the Trustees have acted by a Chairman, who presides at all their meetings; the duty of the President or Vice-President being merely to preside at the annual meetings of the Corporation. The earliest record-book of the Trustees is a little volume, of about five inches by eight, of the poorest and cheapest paper and covers, containing a hundred and sixty pages. It forms an amusing contrast with its more brilliant successors. It embraces the period from 1813 to 1817 inclusive.

February 23, 1813. At the first meeting of the Trustees held at the house of Colonel T. H. Perkins, the draft of an address to the public was read, adopted, and ordered to be printed, "with a suitable circular letter to every clergyman in the Commonwealth."

January 9, 1814. An address to the public, having been approved by the overseers of the poor, was adopted, and Committees appointed to solicit subscriptions.

February 24, 1814. By act of Legislature the Corporation was authorized to grant annuities on lives. In a charter, subsequently granted to the Massachusetts Hospital Life Insurance Company, a proviso was inserted, by which one third of its whole net profits from insurance on lives is made payable to the Hospital.

An additional act, passed January 17, 1824, sanctions a most important agreement between these two Corporations, by which the Hospital, in lieu of all former rights, became entitled to one-third of all the earnings of said Insurance Company, over and above six per cent.

[Note: — Sec. 146, Chap. 119, of the Public Statutes, reads: —

"Every company empowered to make insurance on lives upon land shall be subject to the same obligations for the payment of a certain share of the profits to the Massachusetts General Hospital as are imposed on the Massachusetts Hospital Life-Insurance Company."]

March 25, 1816. Messrs. Quincy and J. L. Sullivan were appointed a Committee to draft a new address to the public. On April 14, the address was ordered to be printed in pamphlet form; and, on April 21, a thousand copies of it were directed to be prepared for distribution. The Board resolved itself, at this last meeting, into Sub-committees for subscriptions.

December 18, 1816. The Board decided to purchase part of Mr. Joy's land. [Site of M'Lean Hospital at Somerville.]

December 29, 1816. The Ward Committees met with the Board of Trustees, and reported *that in three days the subscriptions were* $78,802. Committees for the towns of Salem, Beverly, New Bedford, Plymouth, Charlestown, Medford, Cambridge, Roxbury, and Newburyport, were also appointed. Charles Bulfinch, Esq., was employed to visit the Hospitals of New York, Philadelphia and Baltimore. Meetings now began to be held at the Athenæum, having before been held at the houses of the officers.

January 5, 1817. The subscriptions had increased to $93,969. Authority was given to purchase more of Mr. Joy's land, not exceeding in all fifteen acres, or to cost over fifteen thousand dollars. On January 12, the Committee reported a purchase from Mr. Joy for $15,650; and the Board approved of their Committee's act, though they had somewhat exceeded their powers.

January 19, 1817. A salary was given to the Secretary of a hundred dollars.

February 2, 1817. An address to the public was adopted to obviate an impression that the Insane Hospital was designed exclusively for the wealthy.

March 9, 1817. The Treasurer was invited to attend all the meetings. Public notice was ordered on selection of Superintendent for Asylum. The Committee on the subject of granting annuities reported against the measure.

March 16, 1817. The deed of Benjamin Joy was produced, and the Secretary ordered to buy a tin case to keep it in. It is still [1851] extant, and used for holding the title-deeds.

Mr. Bulfinch presented a ground-plan for an Insane Hospital.

March 23, 1817. The Committee reported that they had examined several sites [for a General Hospital], and were pleased with one in North Allen Street, and arranged that the Board should visit it. Charles Bulfinch sent in a plan for a General Hospital.

March 30, 1817. Each Trustee approved of the site in Allen Street.

April 6, 1817. Medical and Surgical Staff appointed for the General Hospital.

April 20, 1817. A letter from Hon. William Phillips announced his readiness to pay his subscription of twenty thousand dollars, as soon as the town would discharge him, as executor of his father's will, from the five thousand dollars given thereby.

May 4, 1817. The Committee for building an Asylum reported in favor of two wings or buildings, seventy-six feet by forty, three stories high instead of one, and of brick instead of stone. Authority was given to buy the Allen-street Estate at twenty thousand dollars, if the offer should be accepted in six days.

June 12, 1817. By a resolve passed by the Legislature, it is provided that the stone for the erection of the Hospital should be hammered and fitted for use by the convicts in the State Prison. The work thus done is estimated at over thirty thousand dollars.

October 6, 1817. After various delays and negotiations, the Committee reported "the Allen-street purchase as substantially complete."

The purchase of the land in Boston had been attended with great difficulties, and was a most fortunate arrangement for the institution. Negotiations for the purchase of this estate were opened with James S. Colburn, Esq., acting for the Prince heirs, who were supposed to be sole owners; and he once or twice increased the price which he had originally demanded. It was then ascertained that certain others (heirs of the Wells family) had an interest which must be extinguished. A street which had been laid out for the benefit of the Canal Bridge, in continuation of Bridge Street, and respecting the laying out of which some informality had been discovered, was shut up. And still there remained a serious objection, that part of the land had been set off on execution in 1781, on a judgment for £741, against one Hezekiah Blanchard; the sheriff making a general return, that the appraisers were *appointed according to law*, instead of stating specially which of them was chosen by the creditor, debtor, and sheriff respectively. The land was appraised at only about half the debt (£430). The debtor was for years afterwards supported by the creditor, and died a pauper, and was buried at his expense. Strong as was the equity of the case, the legal title of this lot (making an important part of the estate) was bad. Mr. Lowell, an excellent lawyer, and a most influential member of the Committee, was opposed to completing the purchase on the ground of this objection. Messrs. Francis, Quincy, and others of the Committee, were willing to take the risk. Mr. Lowell left for Europe, and his colleagues decided to buy. It is an interesting circumstance, that, just before the end of the forty years allowed by law, Charles G. Loring, Esq., was employed to institute a suit for Benjamin Gray and his sister, as the heirs of the old owner; which was favorably compromised, in part doubtless through Mr. Loring's good offices; the Hospital paying five hundred dollars, and an intervening warrantor paying five hundred more. This same demandant subsequently recovered an estate in Atkinson Street for breach of condition, under circumstances so inequitable, that the suit, as reported in the books (Gray *v.* Blanchard), is known as *the atrocious case;* and the Court avowed that they intentionally postponed giving their opinion, in hopes that the delay would have led to a compromise. Mr. Gray knew no higher standard of right or of duty than "the statute in such case made and provided." He at first refused to accept the Hospital's offer of one thousand dollars. The case was opened to the jury; and Benjamin Gorham, Esq., counsel for the Hospital, began to exhibit him in so unenviable a light, that he intimated his readiness to take the sum offered. The case was thereupon withdrawn from the jury. But for this arrangement, the Hospital would have been put to great inconvenience, if not loss. This possible consequence certainly goes far to justify Mr. Lowell's objections, while the actual result fully warrants the decision of his associates.

This estate, independently of improvements, is now [1851] probably worth at least about three hundred thousand dollars. It cost less than a twelfth of that sum.

November 3, 1817. The Committee reported the draft of an advertisement, offering a hundred dollars' reward for a plan of a Hospital.

November 24, 1817. A common seal was ordered to be prepared; and, on November 30, Colonel May laid it before the Board, — the device being an Indian with his bow in one hand, and an arrow in the other; and on his right a star, being encircled with the inscription, "MASSACHUSETTS GENERAL HOSPITAL, 1811"; and it was accepted accordingly.

December 7, 1817. It was ordered that the Hospital be "of stone, and *of that kind called granite.*"

January 4, 1818. Several plans were received by the Board; and on January 11, referred to a Committee. On January 25 the Committee reported that the plan of a Hospital by Mr. Bulfinch deserved the premium; and on February 1, Mr. Bulfinch's plan (with slight modifications suggested by the Committee) was adopted, and immediate measures were directed for getting stone hammered at the State Prison.

The result of this period, then, was that subscriptions were secured to the amount required by the condition of the charter, and the estates were purchased where the two departments of the institution are now situated. [The M'Lean Hospital has since been moved to Waverley.] The subscriptions had been extremely generous. William Phillips, as we have seen, increased his father's legacy of five thousand dollars to the sum of twenty thousand. The importance of this donation can hardly be over-estimated. It encouraged the friends of the project, and awakened a corresponding liberality in others. It is not too much to say, that it was the one circumstance which insured the success of the undertaking. The Humane Society gave five thousand dollars; Messrs. James Perkins, Thomas H. Perkins, and David Sears, each gave the same sum.

There were in all one thousand and forty-seven subscribers, residing in Boston, Salem, Plymouth, Charlestown, Hingham, and Chelsea (including a few residents elsewhere); and 245 of this number, by giving one hundred dollars and upwards, became members of the Corporation.

A donation-book, prepared in 1828 by Colonel Joseph May, includes these subscriptions, and some subsequent ones, making in all the truly magnificent total of more than a hundred and forty thousand dollars.

March 15, 1818. The Board decided that it is expedient to unite in one person the offices of Physician and Superintendent of the Asylum.

July 4, 1818. The corner-stone of the Hospital in North Allen Street, was laid in Masonic form by the Grand Lodge of Massachusetts. [Pages 38 to 44 (inclusive) of the History are devoted to the proceedings on this occasion.]

September 15, 1818. Visiting Committees were arranged, each to be of three members, and to serve for three months.

November 15, 1818. The Visiting Committee were directed

to hasten the delivery of the stone from State Prison, "that the roof of the Hospital may be covered in as soon as possible."

November 23, 1818. The Visiting Committee report nine patients received at Asylum. Mr. Francis states that he well remembers the admission of the first patient. A father asked to have his son received as an inmate; and the Committee spent three hours in conversing with him, in order to learn all the particulars of the case. He informed them that he believed his son to be one of those spoken of in the Bible as "possessed with a devil"; and, when asked what remedial measures he had adopted, replied that he was in the habit of whipping him. The young man was entirely cured, and became subsequently a pedler, in which vocation he displayed so much Yankee shrewdness, that he acquired a property of ten or twelve thousand dollars. Three hours' deliberation on the admission of each patient would hardly be found practicable in these later times, when the institution numbers two hundred inmates.

July 1, 1819. Thanks were presented to Mr. William H. Lane for the present of a mahogany medicine case, valued at two hundred dollars.

December 19, 1819. Benjamin Wiggin, Esq., offered a celebrated picture, "The Capuchin Chapel," to be exhibited for benefit of the Hospital, and was thanked for "his very generous offer." At a subsequent meeting, April 18, 1820, a Committee was appointed to thank Mr. Wiggin for the $1,604, net proceeds of the exhibition of his picture.

January 6, 1820. Mr. William Hall presented "his patent for sweeping chimneys," to be used in the Hospital.

October 22, 1820. The Building Committee were ordered to take measures to erect the western wing of Hospital in the ensuing spring. They reported that the centre and easterly wing were now nearly finished, but that it was inexpedient to open the Hospital immediately for the reception of patients.

February 11, 1821. It was ordered that Visiting Committees should hereafter consist of two instead of three members, and the term of service of each Committee be two months instead of four.

February 15, 1821. An act of the Legislature exonerates from performance of military duty certain officers of the Hospital; and a like exemption is provided for by the Revised Statutes, passed in 1836.

March 21, 1821. At the annual meeting, a new draft of by-laws was adopted and recorded.

April 29, 1821. It was voted to discontinue meetings on Sunday; which, however, were resumed in 1822.

August 21, 1821. Notice was ordered to Drs. Jackson and Warren that the Hospital will be ready for patients on September 1.

September 3, 1821. One patient was admitted; and, until September 20, not a single other application was made for admission.

December 23, 1821. A model of a machine, called a "goutframe," invented by Mr. Joseph Trumball [Trumbull] for the purpose of moving helpless people to and from bed, was presented.

January 10, 1822. Six free beds were established; three for medical, three for surgical patients.

April 21, 1822. The Building Committee were ordered to take measures for finishing the portico or pediment of the Hospital.

September 1, 1822. A nomination of an Apothecary, as successor to Dr. Green, was made by the Physician and Surgeon; and they were requested "*to withdraw the same, and to nominate some other person.*"

November 10, 1822. A bedstead and other articles, made expressly for the late Abraham Touro during his illness, were presented by his sister.

December 1, 1822. Committee appointed to wait on Hon. William Phillips [President of the Corporation and Donor of $20,000], to request him to sit for his portrait. This portrait by Stuart is, it is needless to say, a fine painting and an excellent likeness.

January, 1823. At the annual meeting, the Trustees reported that the interior of the west wing of the Hospital was finished, and ready for occupation; and that the colonnade in front would be raised in the ensuing season.

February 2, 1823. Committee appointed to subscribe for stock in the Massachusetts Hospital Life Insurance Company, not exceeding fifty thousand dollars. The Committee subscribed for the whole sum named.

February 23, 1823. Messrs. Lyman and Guild were appointed a Committee for collecting a library for each department of the institution.

March 9, 1823. A donation of three hundred dollars for the use of the Asylum was offered and accepted on condition, that, if the donor were ever subsequently to need it, the same should be repaid to him without interest. March 23, one hundred dollars more was offered and accepted on the same condition. On August 10, the donor of the four hundred dollars *on condition* was declared to be Mr. Lambert, of Roxbury, then deceased.

May 4, 1823. A mummy from Thebes was presented by Bryant P. Tilden and Robert B. Edes, in behalf of Jacob Van Lennep and Company, of Smyrna (the Hospital paying two hundred dollars out of the proceeds of its exhibition to the Boston Dispensary), which was gratefully accepted. This mummy is now [1899] an appropriate ornament of the [old] operating room at the Hospital.

The profits of the exhibition of the mummy are stated to be fifteen hundred dollars. The donation-book, probably deducting certain charges and the payment to the Dispensary, makes the sum but little less than twelve hundred dollars.

October 7, 1823. The Committee reported that they had leased the mummy one year for exhibition in other cities. The Chairman reported that the portrait of the President [William Phillips; by Stuart, then sixty-seven years old] was finished; and, on October 10, it was received. The west wing of the Hospital was now ready for patients.

November 2, 1823. The gratifying announcement was made of a bequest from John M'Lean, of twenty-five thousand dollars, payable on death of his widow, and with the information that he had also made this institution his residuary legatee, by which "a much larger sum" would be secured. This residue proved to be over ninety thousand dollars.

Mr. M'Lean was a truly noble specimen of a Boston merchant. Having many years before failed in business, he settled with all his creditors, and obtained a full discharge. Soon afterwards, by the safe arrival, as I believe, of a vessel supposed to have been lost, he retrieved his affairs. He forthwith called a meeting of his creditors, and paid to each of them the balance due, both principal and interest.

November 23, 1823. A Committee was appointed to obtain a portrait of Mr. M'Lean [Donor of $119,858.20], and to report on the expediency of obtaining portraits of other liberal donors. On December 7, the Committee for obtaining Mr. M'Lean's portrait were also charged with procuring a portrait of the late Samuel Eliot [Donor of $10,000].

February 8, 1824. Messrs. Francis and Guild were appointed a Committee on the settlement of accounts by the executors of Mr. M'Lean, as to the amount charged for commissions, and the investment of the trust-fund.

In the ninth volume of Pickering's Reports, page 447, is a report of the suit brought by Harvard College and the Hospital v. the surviving Trustee under Mr. M'Lean's will; in which the Court decided that the Trustees had the right to select any stocks they pleased for the trust-fund. They had appropriated to this object insurance stock, entitled to large foreign claims, and manufacturing stocks, which shortly afterwards made large dividends for sale of patent rights and patterns and machinery. The two Corporations had offered to pay six per cent interest to the widow (three thousand dollars a year) in December, 1823; but their proposal was declined. The ultimate value of the trust-property received on the decease of Mrs. M'Lean, in the year 1834, was thus reduced to less than twenty thousand dollars for each of the two Corporations, while she herself received an income probably averaging twelve per cent per annum. It is believed that every Trustee of the Hospital and every Corporator of the College coincided in opinion, that this investment of the trust-funds, though adjudged to be legal, was not made in the exercise of a sound discretion, and with a due regard to the rights of all parties.

February 20, 1824. A patient was dismissed by the Visiting Committee "for having introduced liquor privately."

April 9, 1824. Thanks were given to Gorham Parsons, Esq., *"for the present of a sow of an uncommonly fine breed.'* Her weight, in the Visiting Committee's records, is stated at 273 pounds. As this gift is noticed in both records, it evidently made a great sensation.

June 6, 1824. A cold and warm salt-water bathing-house was ordered to be erected at the Hospital.

January 7, 1825. Committees were appointed to procure portraits of Mr. [Thomas] Oliver [Donor of $22,438.70] and Mr. [Abraham] Touro [Donor of $10,300]. The portrait of John M'Lean was brought in at this meeting. It is one of the happiest works of Stuart. The record says of this painting, " The resemblance is striking, and the expression characteristic."

June 20, 1825. General Lafayette, with his son and several gentlemen, accompanied by his Excellency the Governor and the Lieutenant-Governor, visited the Hospital. They were received by the President of the Corporation, the Board of Trustees, and the Physicians and Surgeons, and were conducted through the several wards and other parts of the building.

October 7, 1825. It was voted that the Visiting Committees should make their visits unattended by the superintendents, apothecaries, or nurses, probably in order that patients might more freely state any causes of complaint.

October 23, 1825. An important vote was passed, placing a free bed for one year at the disposal of any one who should pay one hundred dollars.

November 6, 1825. A quarterly analysis of the accounts, showing the cost of stores, &c., was ordered to be laid before the Board.

December 18, 1825. The fact that certain persons were in the habit of visiting the Hospital on Sundays, and having religious worship in the wards, often producing an unfavorable excitement in the patients, was communicated to the Board; and the subject was referred to the Chairman and Mr. Prescott, who, by a written report at the next meeting, put an end to the practice alluded to.

January 12, 1826. A Committee (by Mr. Francis, the Chairman) reported in favor of receiving actual possession now of Thomas Oliver's property ($24,138.70), and agreeing to pay his widow thirteen hundred dollars a year during her life; which report was accepted.

February 5, 1826. An extra grant was made to Dr. Wyman of five hundred dollars for his services and aid in regard to the new building at the Asylum.

April 7, 1826. A free bed for life was placed at the disposal of Mrs. Ann M'Lean, widow of John M'Lean, Esq.

May 21, 1826. The Committee on Mr. Eliot's portrait reported that it was painted by Mr. Stuart, and had been placed at the Asylum. [Removed to Hospital, October 10, 1826.]

June 12, 1826. The Committee appointed at the last meeting of the Corporation, to take into consideration the best mode of perpetuating the memory of John M'Lean, recommended that the Asylum be hereafter known as "The M'Lean Asylum for the Insane"; which report was accepted and ordered to be laid before the Corporation. The report itself is copied on the records of the Corporation. It closes as follows: "Your Committee have reason to believe, from the information of one of their number, that the proposed arrangement will be entirely satisfactory to the friends of the testator and benefactor."

The contingency had now occurred, which was contemplated in the charter, of a donation greater than that of the Commonwealth. It was the feeling of Mrs. M'Lean, and also, at first, of others of the testator's connections, that the corporate name should be changed.

There was an earnest desire to do all that could or ought to be done to express the high sense entertained of this act of munificence. The decision finally made was, it is believed, alike expedient for the Hospital, and just to the deceased. His name was given to one of the two great departments of the institution, on which a very large sum was forthwith expended for the erection of additional buildings, and where many expensive improvements have since been made, so that the actual cost of the establishment which bears his name is more than double the amount realized from his whole bequest. On the other hand, the corporate name remaining unchanged, many sons and daughters of Massachusetts have since contributed to it as a *State* institution, what perhaps they would have hesitated to bestow, if it had borne the name of a private founder.

October 6, 1826. John Welles, Esq., offered trees and shrubs from his place at Dorchester, for the use of the Hospital; also the loan of his teams, plough, and driver, to put the grounds in order.

November 29, thanks were given to Hon. John Welles and Hon. Jonathan Hunnewell, for a large number of young trees and ornamental shrubs.

January 9, 1827. Erysipelatous inflammation having appeared at Hospital, the expediency of removing all the patients was discussed; and four Trustees were appointed a Committee on the subject. January 14, the Committee reported that they had decided, after conference with the Physician and Surgeon, to make a temporary removal of all patients from the Hospital (as far as practicable) with a view to a "thorough purification by fumigation or otherwise;" and that the Rev. Dr. James Freeman has very liberally and readily offered his dwelling-house in Vine Street, near the Hospital, for the accommodation of the patients. January 21, twelve patients were reported as removed to Dr. Freeman's house, and twenty-one discharged. January 28, the Hospital was reported to be entirely clear of patients, and "cleansing, fumigation, and alteration of fire-places, &c., in progress." February 4, the patients from Dr. Freeman's house were received back into the Hospital. March 25, Dr. Robbins was appointed a Committee to return to Dr. Freeman the key of his house, with thanks.

September 2, 1827. The portrait of Mr. [William] Phillips was at this meeting loaned to the Trustees of Phillips Academy.

December 16, 1827. The Visiting Committee, appointed at the last meeting, reported on the subject of rates of board at the Asylum, that they should never be less than three dollars nor more than twelve dollars per week. By special vote, subsequently, some have paid at rates as low as two dollars, and as high as twenty dollars per week.

January 11, 1828. The Superintendent was directed not to buy any more "domestic coffee." The nature of this "villanous compound" is not stated on the records; but it was probably a preparation of rye.

March 9, 1828. Colonel May was requested to prepare a list of all donations to the Massachusetts General Hospital, and one hundred dollars was appropriated to that object. This vote is the origin of the "Donation-book," decidedly the most important of all the records of the institution.

April 11, 1828. Dr. Wyman was authorized to procure a carriage and a pair of horses, to be used at the M'Lean Asylum for the Insane, for the purpose of giving air and exercise to the boarders.

A grant of one hundred dollars was made to Mr. and Mrs. Gurney, "for their kind, assiduous, and faithful services as Superintendent and Matron of the Hospital."

April 27, 1828. Mr. Greenough applying to buy the reversionary interest of the Corporation in the Province House Estate, Messrs. Francis and Lawrence were appointed a Committee to ascertain its value. The Hospital declined making the proposed sale.

July 8, 1828. The Secretary was directed henceforth to audit the accounts of both branches of the institution, with a salary of one hundred dollars additional for that duty.

July 11, 1828. The cylindrical tin case, containing the title-deeds, &c., was deposited in the safe of the Massachusetts Hospital Life Insurance Company.

[In March, 1844, it was again restored to the Treasurer's custody.]

August 3, 1828. The Board declined, "though with sincere regret," loaning the portraits of their donors for an exhibition of " Stuart's Pictures." [Mr. Stuart died July, 1828.]

September 7, 1828. The apothecary was ordered to be styled the House Physician.

October 26, 1828. Mr. Francis and the Visiting Committee were appointed to revise the rules and regulations for the Asylum. On November 11, they made a report, abolishing the office of Steward, and substituting a Clerk and Supervisor, with prescribed duties, with salaries of three hundred and four hundred dollars.

December 14, 1828. A special meeting of the Trustees was held; present, the whole Board, except Dr. Robbins, confined by illness. The record reads : " The present meeting was in consequence of a fire which broke out in the eastern wing of the Hospital, just before the morning service, and which, though at first threatening the destruction of the building, was happily subdued, after causing some injury to the roof and upper apartments." Votes were passed, thanking the fire-department of this and the neighboring towns, which were ordered to be published, with a notice, "that the damage sustained by the building is not so great as to interrupt the reception of patients as usual." It appears that ten convalescent patients were discharged, and all those in the east wards removed to the other part of the house, but without any great " suffering, either from the alarm or the removal." The damage did not exceed six hundred dollars.

February 12, 1829. The Superintendent was ordered to purchase " a suitable number of silver spoons for use at the Hospital, instead of the present pewter ones."

September 27, 1829. John Williams, " a colored man," having been admitted into the Hospital, under permit of Dr. George W. Otis [Assistant Surgeon], dated September 19, it was voted that Dr. Otis be requested to state in writing to this Board the circumstances which, in his opinion, constituted this a case of emergency within the meaning of second article of second chapter of the rules and regulations.

October 9, Dr. Otis's answer was received, stating that he had never before seen a copy of the rules and regulations, and that he did *not* think the case referred to was one of emergency within the meaning of those rules.

November 22, 1829. General Cobb being now a patient in the Hospital, where he subsequently died, a bill of Dr. Channing [Assistant Physician] for extra services rendered him was referred to the Visiting Committee, who, after consultation with Drs. Jackson and Channing, approved the same.

February 21, 1830. Mr. Gurney's intended marriage was announced, and the subject was referred to Dr. Robbins and the Visiting Committee. March 21, Mr. Gurney announced that his intended wife had consented to reside at the Hospital. The wedding was subsequently celebrated in fine style; the House Physicians, &c., officiating as groomsmen. Many patients were present at the wedding visit. It was a gay scene, — one seldom witnessed in a Hospital. [NOTE. Mr. Nathan Gurney was Superintendent at the Hospital from 1825 to 1833. His former wife had died March 7, 1829.]

Messrs. Gray, Ticknor, and the Secretary were appointed a Committee to make an entirely new draft of the rules and regulations; whose reports were accepted, May 9 and 23, for the Hospital and Asylum respectively. They were prepared with great care and labor, each paragraph being discussed and considered, and the whole being finally read by the Trustees, and by the Physicians and Surgeons. These rules and regulations are recorded *in extenso*, occupying twenty pages. One important change introduced was, that, though each Trustee should serve for two months on the Visiting Committee, one Trustee should go out each month, so that there should always be one member of the Committee informed of the existing state of affairs.

October 21, 1830. A letter from Thomas Lee, administrator of Francis Lee, a deceased patient, was received and read, communicating a gift from his father, Joseph Lee, Esq., sole heir of said deceased, of twenty thousand dollars for the use of the Asylum ($250 a year, for four years, to be paid to Dr. Wyman). It was thereupon voted to accept this munificent donation; and Messrs. Lawrence, Guild, and the Secretary were appointed a Committee to communicate to Mr. Lee "the grateful acknowledgments of the Board."

This donation consisted of twelve shares in the Eliot Manufacturing Company, and of eight shares in the Merrimack Company, under the restriction not to sell the same for ten years, except with the consent of Joseph Lee, Esq.

December 5, a letter was received from Dr. Wyman, declining the donation of Mr. Lee, on the general and high-minded ground of the impropriety of receiving presents from any boarder or his friends.

February 13, 1831. Messrs. Francis and Lawrence were appointed a Committee to wait on Miss Mary Belknap [Donor of $89,882.60], sister of Jeremiah Belknap, Esq. [Donor of $10,100], and on the relatives of Joseph Lee, Esq. [Donor of $20,000], to ask for their portraits; and said Committee, at the next meeting, reported that "no portraits of Mr. Belknap or Mr. Lee are in possession of their relatives."

It is a curious fact that a portrait of Mr. Belknap was painted for the Hospital by the late [1851] Henry Sargent, *from looking at Mr. Head.* Mr. Belknap and Mr. Head, at a certain hour of each day, often walked together; and Mr. Sargent, to refresh his recollection of how Mr. Belknap used to look, was in the habit of going out and meeting Mr. Head when he was walking alone, that his imagination and his pencil might be thus aided in recalling the features of Mr. Head's former companion. The likeness is by no means perfect; yet, I think, all who knew Mr. Belknap would feel sure that it was intended for him.

June 13, 1832. [Annual meeting.] The annual meeting was altered to the fourth Wednesday in January; so that the Trustees now chosen served only about six months.

December 14, 1832. Mr. Francis informs me, that one of the young medical men selected to assist Dr. Wyman in keeping his accounts (several years before this period) received the appointment, principally because the Trustees were delighted with his letter of application, which was the most exquisite specimen of penmanship that they had ever beheld. He entered on his duties, and was found to write a most illegible hand. He was asked whether that letter was his own unaided composition. He replied that it was. "But," added he, "I did not *write* it, — I *painted* it." It was, indeed, the elaborate production of an *artist*, executed with great delicacy by means of a *hair-pencil*.

February 17, 1833. Richard S. Roberts applied for leave to remove a blind placed against the window of his house in Fruit Court, overlooking the Hospital Garden. July 5, Mr. Roberts was allowed to have a window with a reversed blind.

October 8, 1833. Benjamin D. Greene, Esq., resigned his situation as a Trustee, in view of an intended absence in Europe. He was, however, re-elected the ensuing year.

January 8, 1834. A memorial from the Physicians and Surgeons as to a new building or wing at the Hospital was received and referred. Eleven years afterwards, such a building was erected.

April 16, 1834. It was directed that the head of the Asylum be known as the Physician and Superintendent.

July 11, 1834. The application of Eliza Bryant for leave to erect a building on Fruit Street, with windows opening on the Hospital-ground, was declined.

July 20, 1834. A very elaborate and excellent report from Mr. Eliot was entered on the records, defining the relative duties of the Superintendent and of the Physicians, &c., of the Hospital. It concludes thus: "Much must be left to the discretion of those who hold responsible stations; and, having expressed their general views of the subject — having stated, as it were, their theory of the government of the institution, — the Trustees must leave the application of them to the good sense and good feelings of the present incumbents, with the single intimation, that they consider harmony of action in the officers essential to the prosperity of the Hospital."

January 9, 1835. "Whereas Dr. Wyman has repeatedly and earnestly requested to be relieved from his arduous and responsible duties as soon as the interests of the M'Lean Asylum will admit, and the Trustees feel it a duty to him to fix a time for his retirement, in order to give him an opportunity to make suitable arrangements for the future, — voted, that his resignation be respectfully accepted, to take effect on May 1 next. Voted, that, in consideration of his long, zealous, and unwearied exertions during sixteen years, — in the commencement of an institution then novel in this part of the country, and in conducting it to its present prosperous state, — the sum of one thousand dollars be granted to him and paid by the Treasurer."

November 8, 1835. It was voted that the thanks of the Board be presented to the executors of Mrs. Prescott for the portrait of their late distinguished benefactor, Thomas Oliver, Esq. Mrs. Prescott was his widow; and the portrait thus given is in the Trustees' room at the Hospital. It is not a fine painting, and is said not to be a very good likeness. It is, however, valuable as being a portrait taken from life, of and for himself, and the only one which has been preserved.

January 8, 1836. Messrs. Gray, Eliot, and Quincy were appointed a Committee to draw up the annual report. The report, as prepared by Mr. Gray, had in a striking degree the merit of brevity. It was one sentence of six lines, purporting, without any comment, to present certain annexed reports from the two departments of the institution.

Among these documents, however, was a very important and valuable one from Dr. Lee, describing minutely the system of occupation, diversion, and moral management at the Asylum; the Belknap Sewing Society; the weekly dancing parties; the religious service on the Sabbath, &c.

June 5, 1836. The price of free beds for life was fixed at such a sum as would be required by the annuity tables to purchase an annuity of one hundred dollars.

July 5, 1836. Mr. Eliot was appointed a Committee to confer with Dr. Lee, " to hire or purchase a piano-forte for the Asylum, with appropriate music." Mr. Eliot and Mr. Lawrence were chosen a Committee to purchase a billiard table for the Asylum, if they should consider it expedient. Both were purchased.

October 7, 1836. At a quarterly meeting, *no member of the Board made his appearance.*

October 30, 1836. At a special meeting of the Trustees, called on the occasion of Dr. Lee's death, resolutions were adopted, and a vote expressive of their sympathy for his widow, and for defraying all expenses of his last illness, and payment of his salary to April 1; also a vote inviting the widow to remain at the Asylum as long as she might think proper.

November 6, 1836. The Superintendent was directed " to call on Mr. Tappan, and inform him that it will not be convenient to receive into the Hospital the colored man proposed to be sent by him."

December 11, 1836. Dr. Luther V. Bell was unanimously elected Physician and Superintendent of the Asylum, "provided a Committee then appointed, consisting of Messrs. Eliot and Quincy, shall be satisfied that he will pursue the course of moral and religious treatment of patients adopted by Dr. Lee, and they shall be so satisfied before communicating the appointment." December 16, the Committee reported the acceptance of Dr. Bell.

February 19, 1837. A grant of $250 was made to Mr. and Mrs. Columbus Tyler [Steward and Matron], for their extra services, under their increased and arduous duties, resulting from the sudden decease of Dr. Lee, Physician and Superintendent at the Asylum.

April 23, 1837. The Visiting Committee, Messrs. Lawrence and Eliot, reported the following vote, drawn up by Mr. Eliot, which was adopted: "Voted that the Trustees have recently seen, with great pain, that a violation of the rules of the institution by one of its officers has become the subject of newspaper animadversion. In an institution like this, to which it is so difficult to attract, and in which it is so important to command, public confidence, the strictest and most scrupulous adherence to rules, of which the propriety is unquestioned, is required by a just regard as well to its usefulness to the public, as to the character of those who have any agency in its direction and control. Where many persons are connected in different departments, the reputation of all is more or less affected by the conduct of each; and all are therefore bound, by respect for others as well as themselves, to conduct in such a manner as to give no reasonable ground for complaint. The Trustees have felt unlimited confidence that no officer of the institution would expose himself to just censure, and they have on all occasions been but very slightly affected by remarks which they have had reason to believe were founded on jealousy or misconception. But it is with very different feelings they regard an accusation of violation of rule, which, on inquiry, proves to be true; and they think it due to themselves to take serious notice of it, and to put on record their denial of all knowledge of the circumstance at the time of its occurrence, and to express their hope that nothing may ever again require a similar expression of their feelings. Lest, however, the breach of confidence may be imagined to be of a more serious character than it really was, they think proper to state, that the circumstance to which they allude was the employment of Dr. J. Mason Warren, a young man not connected with the Hospital, during the absence of his father, whose turn it was to officiate;" and a copy of this vote was sent to all the Surgeons of the Hospital.

When it is remembered, that Dr. John C. Warren had been Surgeon of the Hospital from its foundation, — that the Board had not the slightest distrust of the capacity of his son to perform the duties alluded to, it must be admitted, that the preceding vote is an honorable proof of their vigilance and independence. This son was a few years afterwards appointed one of the Surgeons of the Hospital, the duties of which station he has discharged with signal ability and success. A reply from Dr. Warren, which was of the most candid, manly, and appropriate character, was received at the next meeting.

This censure, alike given and received in a proper spirit, did but tend thenceforth to strengthen and confirm between both parties feelings of mutual confidence, regard, and respect.

October 13, 1837. A communication from Dr. James Jackson, by which he resigned his situation as one of the Physicians of the Hospital, having been read, the following votes, submitted by Mr. Bowditch, were unanimously adopted; viz.,

"Voted that the Trustees have learned this determination of Dr. Jackson with the utmost regret. Connected as he has been with the institution from its first establishment, they are well aware how much he has always done to raise and maintain its reputation, and to extend its usefulness. Possessing the purest and most exemplary private character, with talents and attainments which have placed him at the head of his profession, and with kind and affable manners which have won the affections of his patients and conciliated the esteem and good-will of his associates, the Trustees cannot but regard his retirement from the Hospital as a most severe and serious loss. While they accept his resignation, therefore, they avail themselves of the opportunity publicly to acknowledge that he was among the most active and influential of the original founders of the Hospital; that, by an uniform course of disinterested professional and personal service, he has ever been one of its ablest officers and best friends; and that he is thus, in their opinion, entitled to the lasting gratitude of the institution and of the community. Voted, also, that, as a testimonial of the respect of the Trustees for Dr. Jackson, a free bed in the Hospital be placed at his disposal during life."

December 17, 1837. A letter from Dr. [James] Jackson was received, and the Chairman and Mr. Eliot were appointed a Committee to procure his portrait or bust as they may see fit.

April 18, 1838. A billiard-table was ordered for the female patients at the Asylum.

September 16, 1838. Messrs. Lamb and Bowditch were appointed a Committee on the subject of a bequest of the late Ambrose S. Courtis; to whom was also referred, on September 30, a proposal of the heirs at law for a compromise. Pursuant to a subsequent report of this Committee, one quarter part of the bequest was accepted in full (two thousand five hundred dollars), provided no greater percentage be paid to any other legatee.

January 23, 1839. At this annual meeting of the Corporation was passed the vote by which all persons who have served, or shall hereafter serve, as Trustees, are to be considered members of the Corporation.

March 24, 1839. Measures were ordered to protect the Hospital-garden against claims of air and light from windows opening thereon.

October 11, 1839. Messrs. Shaw and Brimmer were instructed to report as to the expediency of rejecting syphilitic patients, or of charging them extra board; and this Committee subsequently reported, that such patients should be received only in urgent cases, and should always be charged double the usual rates of board; and this rule has ever since been acted on.

Messrs. Bond and Bowditch were appointed a Committee to consider the expediency of applying to the Surgeons for the records, or for leave to copy the same, who at a subsequent meeting reported in favor of such an application. The Physicians had always regarded their records as the property of the institution. Dr. Warren, on the contrary, considered the surgical records as his own private memoranda. The appointment of this Committee, however, and their suggestions as to the importance of the institution's possessing either the originals of these records or copies of them, induced him very cheerfully to yield up any private claim.

October 23, 1839. It having been announced to the Board, that Gamaliel Bradford, M. D., Superintendent of the Massachusetts General Hospital, died on Tuesday forenoon, six months' additional salary was granted to Mrs. Bradford; and she and her family were invited to remain at the Hospital till the choice of a new Superintendent. Mrs. Bradford was, by a special vote, subsequently continued in the office of Matron till the first of April following.

November 3, 1839. At this meeting, the Committee upon the records of cases made their formal report which was accepted; and the House Physician and Surgeon were directed, for the future, to record all cases in volumes to be prepared for that purpose.

December 29, 1839. The Visiting Committee were authorized "to procure a water-bed, if they think proper."

May 17, 1840. The rules as to the admission of students at the Hospital were modified; and it was made henceforth the duty of the Physicians and Surgeons to nominate two persons as House Physician and two as House Surgeon, one of these nominees to be subsequently chosen by the Trustees.

July 15, 1840. The officer called House Apothecary at the Asylum was ordered to be known as the Assistant Physician.

mber 7, 1841. Dr. [John C.] Warren transmitted a letter enclosing one thousand dollars as a fund for the purchase of religious and moral books to be given to patients on leaving the Hospital. This donation was accepted; and Dr. Warren was thanked "for his early, efficient, and continued interest in this institution;" his letter being recorded *in extenso*.

May 3, 1842. At a special meeting, it was voted, that the Trustees, under "their feeling of great anxiety from the introduction of the small-pox and varioloid into the General Hospital, hereby recommend, that, until these diseases are expelled, as few patients as possible be admitted into the Hospital; and that all patients who are admitted shall be first informed of the condition of the house; and that the Visiting Committee be requested to inform the Physicians and Surgeons of this opinion of the Trustees, and to urge upon them to give such care and directions as shall in their judgment be most effectual to prevent these diseases from spreading among the patients."

The Visiting Committee and Mr. Dexter were appointed a Committee to cleanse, whitewash and paint the Hospital.

July 15, 1842. The Superintendent was directed to prohibit the use of tobacco *by the patients within the house*. It has been since much more stringently and generally excluded.

August 21, 1842. The Treasurer was authorized "to reimburse Mr. Brimmer the cost and expenses incurred by him in procuring the marble bust of Dr. [James] Jackson." This bust is now in the Trustees' room. As a work of art, it is truly admirable. It is the most speaking likeness that can be conceived. It will transmit to coming times the calm and benignant countenance of the first Physician of the Hospital.

March 5, 1843. The Visiting Committee were ordered to confer with Dr. Bell as to procuring a clergyman to officiate at the Asylum. [NOTE. Dr. Bell, in his report for this year, says, " By direction of your Board, an engagement was made early in the year with the Rev. Frederick T. Perkins to preach at the Asylum on the evening of each Sunday. He has discharged the duty acceptably to all parties interested, and we trust that his health and duties will permit a continuance of an arrangement which has proved so useful and interesting to our institution."]

The House Apothecary at Hospital was ordered to be chosen annually, at the time of the choice of Physicians and Surgeons.

March 19, 1843. The Visiting Committee and Mr. Bowditch were appointed a Committee to have tablets prepared with names of the donors, to be placed over such free beds as are supported from their funds, as in the case of the Brimmer and Tucker free beds. This was subsequently found to be very distasteful to patients, as making an odious discrimination between free and pay patients, and was rescinded.

April 2, 1843. Mr. Rogers was appointed a Committee "to complete the list of subscriptions, donations, and legacies, commenced by Col. Joseph May."

July 2, 1843. A box was ordered at the Hospital for preservation of valuable papers. It is now kept in the Trustees' room. [In the attic of the Hospital, 1899.]

December 3, 1843. A communication having been received from William Appleton, enclosing a check for the sum of ten thousand dollars, as a donation for the purpose of affording aid to such patients in the M'Lean Asylum as from straitened means might be compelled to leave the institution without a perfect cure, — it was " voted that the Trustees appreciate highly the liberality and wisdom of this act of charity, and accept this donation to be held sacred for the special purpose designated by the donor."

December 31, 1843. Voted "that the present and past Physicians and Surgeons of the institution be requested to suggest to this Board any changes in the management or arrangements of the Hospital, which in their view would increase its usefulness, and also to express their opinion of the necessity of enlarging the buildings." The result of this vote was the enlargement of the Hospital by the addition of two wings, each fifty feet square.

January 12, 1844. Grants were made of two hundred dollars to Dr. Bell, and one hundred each to Mr. and Mrs. Tyler.

March 31, 1844. Messrs. Rogers and Andrews were appointed a Committee to expend fifty dollars for the formation of a permanent library at the Hospital.

April 12, 1844. Dr. Hale was permitted to erect a pole in the Hospital-grounds for the purpose of a rain-gauge. Messrs. Rogers, Bowditch, and Wigglesworth were appointed a Committee to consider the subject of procuring tablets of the names of benefactors of this institution, and to report thereon to this Board.

This Committee have never yet acted.

April 17, 1844. Messrs. Rogers and Amory were appointed a Committee as to Physicians charging fees to patients able to pay, who subsequently reported in favor of the same in case of out-door patients.

Messrs. Rogers, Amory, Edwards, and Andrews were appointed a Committee to solicit subscriptions for enlarging the Hospital. At the next meeting, May 19, this Committee reported an address to the public, which was adopted. Much of this address is devoted to a description of the original subscription which " was made by persons of all conditions of life, and in sums varying from twenty thousand dollars to twenty-five cents, — the gift of a poor black, whose name, as it deserves, is recorded with others on the books of the donors."

The address closes as follows: —

" To found and maintain institutions for the sick and afflicted is not only the mark but the privilege of civilization; and he who gives evidence of his faithful discharge of duty in this regard will leave a memento of himself, that shall outlive his generation, and be dear to the hearts of his children and of every true man."

[NOTE. The sum of $62,550 was subsequently subscribed for the enlargement of the Hospital.]

June 23, 1844. Mr. Dexter reported plans of two additional wings; the Subscription Committee reported progress; and a Building Committee of five was appointed.

August 18, 1844. Five new rules and regulations were adopted, one of which was, " The smoking of tobacco is prohibited in the premises of the Hospital."

September 15, 1844. Messrs. Andrews and Lamb were appointed a Committee, with full powers, to obtain an engraving of the Asylum. It was executed accordingly.

December 1, 1844. The Butler Hospital, of Rhode Island, asking permission to send Dr. Bell to Europe for some months, Mr. Bowditch was requested to send an answer acceding to their request, and to make the necessary arrangements with Dr. Bell for that purpose. The compliment thus paid to Dr. Bell was truly gratifying, both to him and to this institution. On December 15 he was authorized to engage Dr. Fox to assist Dr. Booth during his absence in Europe.

February 2, 1845. An Annual Committee was constituted to purchase books for distribution under the Warren Fund.

March 30, 1845. Hon. Edward Everett offered to the Hospital his statue of Apollo; and the Trustees presented to him "their grateful acknowledgments for his beautiful gift, valuable as a memorial, that, amidst his arduous public duties in a foreign country [as Minister at the Court of St. James] Mr. Everett feels an undiminished interest in the charitable institutions of his native land."

May 4, 1845. A bequest of one hundred dollars from the late William Russell was transmitted, and gratefully accepted by the Trustees. The money was invested in silver spoons for the Asylum.

September 14, 1845. The Building Committee and Mr. Dexter were instructed to finish the two new wings.

November 2, 1845. Mr. Goodwin having resigned his office of Superintendent of the Hospital, on account of illness, his salary was ordered to be paid to the end of six months after the close of the present quarter.

A Committee were requested to obtain, if possible, portraits of Mr. [Daniel] Waldo [Donor of $40,200] and Mr. [Israel] Munson [Donor of $21,000] for this institution. The portraits of these two donors were procured accordingly, and are now in the Trustees' room at the Hospital, by the side of the earlier benefactors of the institution, the example of whose liberality they had so nobly imitated.

November 26, 1845. A special meeting was held; and the death of Mr. Goodwin, the late Superintendent, was announced.

About a week before Mr. Goodwin's death, I had called to see him. He was seated in an arm-chair, in the Trustees' room. It was one of the most charming days of the "Indian Summer." The south-west wind, cooled by its passage over the water, was admitted freely through the open windows of the apartment. Pleasure carriages and loaded vehicles, in a ceaseless procession, were seen moving rapidly or slowly along the street, and across the bridge to which it led. The river was studded with sail-boats and other vessels. The distant hum of voices, as it arose upon the ear, was drowned by the merry laugh of children just released from the neighboring school. Around us were all the varied activities of a great city, its full tide of business and of happiness.

November 30, 1845. The office of Treasurer, the duties of which had always hitherto been performed gratuitously, had now become very onerous; and it was voted that there should be attached to it henceforth a salary of five hundred dollars.

December 14, 1845. The Committee on Mr. Oliver's tomb reported by Mr. Bowditch, "that said tomb is held by this Corporation, not as their property, but in trust as the burial-place of Mr. Oliver and his family."

February 1, 1846. A Free-bed Standing Committee was appointed.

February 22, 1846. In answer to a communication of Dr. John C. Warren, inquiring the views of this Board as to the erection of a Medical College in this vicinity, a vote was passed "that they cannot perceive any advantage to this institution to arise therefrom."

May 3, 1846. Messrs. Andrews and Dexter were appointed a Committee "to erect a suitable monument to the memory of Jeremiah and Mary Belknap, with full powers."

Five hundred dollars was placed at the disposal of Dr. Bell for the relief of poor patients.

Mr. Dexter reported that the new [west] wing would be ready for occupancy in the present week; and the subject of inviting the benefactors to visit the Hospital was referred to the Visiting Committee. Such an invitation was accordingly issued, and large numbers availed themselves of it.

May 17, 1846. Dr. Bell's expenses to Washington, to attend a late meeting of the Superintendents of Insane Institutions, were ordered to be paid. [Similar expenses, from year to year, have been paid up to the present time, 1899.]

The subject of building a new kitchen, and of ventilating the (old) east wing of the Hospital, was referred to the Building Committee, who reported in favor of both measures; the estimated expense of the kitchen, as reported by Mr. Dexter, being ten thousand dollars. [It cost $16,500.]

October 16, 1846. Books were ordered to be kept as a record of all out-door patients.

NOTE.— On this day " Sulphuric Ether was first used for the prevention of pain to a patient undergoing a serious operation at the Massachusetts General Hospital. This application was made by Mr. W. T. G. Morton. The experiment was a success."*

December 20, 1846. "A letter from Dr. William T. G. Morton offering to the Hospital the right to use his discovery for the alleviation of pain in surgical operations was read; and

---

* From the Address of Welcome, by Charles H. Dalton, Esq., President of the Massachusetts General Hospital, at the commemoration of the Semi-Centennial of Anæsthesia, October 16, 1896.

it was voted that the offer of Dr. Morton be accepted, and that the Secretary be directed to return the thanks of the institution to Dr. Morton in behalf of this Board."

[NOTE. Pages 215 to 348 (inclusive) of Mr. Bowditch's History are devoted to an exhaustive review of the "Ether Discovery."]

February 28, 1847. One of Oberhausser's microscopes was ordered to be purchased for use of Admitting Physician, at the cost of fifty dollars.

April 21, 1847. Five hundred dollars was appropriated towards aiding the poorer patients at the Asylum.

April 26, 1847. Twenty-five dollars was voted towards buying a wooden leg for Ann Kerr, a patient in the Hospital.

May 9, 1847. Messrs. Dexter and Rogers were appointed a Committee respecting a new fence round the Hospital grounds, with directions to ascertain the probable cost, &c.

June 27, 1847. The new east wing being completed, the contributors and the public were invited to visit it. July 16 the entry is made: "The new east wing is now open for the reception of patients."

November 7, 1847. The Visiting Committee reported against the word "free" being added to the tickets over the beds of patients, to distinguish *free* from *pay* patients.

November 21, 1847. A communication from Dr. Henry I. Bowditch, as to the formation of a Medical Library at the Hospital, was referred to Messrs. Rogers and Amory, who subsequently recommended an appropriation of two hundred and fifty dollars for that purpose.

In the Annual Report for 1847 the following mention is made of John Redman's bequest [$137,614.50] : "As the legacy of a Boston mechanic, this will ever be a truly memorable instance of munificence; while its amount entitles the donor to be ranked among the very first benefactors of this institution." The report proceeds: "With no less gratitude have the Trustees acknowledged another legacy of an especially interesting character received within this period. Miss Sarah Clough (for many years a valued and confidential domestic in the family of Joseph W. Revere, Esq., of this city) bequeathed to this institution the residue of her property, the little savings of her own personal labors. The amount which has been paid to the Treasurer, pursuant to this bequest, is $599.84. There never has been a donation, whatever its magnitude, more honorable either to the donor or to the institution."

May 7, 1848. Mrs. Girdler [wife of Superintendent] was requested to purchase a suitable wedding gift to be presented to Thomas W. Hickford and Elizabeth M'Intire, as a token of the appreciation by the Trustees of their long and faithful services at the Hospital.

June 4, 1848. The Building Committee reported, that the new west wing cost $29,500; east wing, $28,000; furnishing, $19,000; repairing centre, rebuilding old east wing cellar throughout, three reservoirs, copper gutters, old kitchen, outside painting, $24,000; new kitchen, $16,500; autopsy-room, sheds, chains, roads, sodding, fences, $3,000: total, $120,000.

June 8, 1849. The Visiting Committee's record states, "Told John Ferris, that, if he was again found smoking in the ward, he would be discharged immediately."

August 12, 1849. The record reads, "An adjourned meeting of the Board was held at the Hospital, after evening service. The Secretary, having recently met with a severe railroad accident, was unable to attend, and desired me to act in his behalf.

At the hour appointed for the meeting, there was a violent storm; and most of the Board pass their summer months in the country. The result was, that not a single member of the Board attended, a circumstance which probably never happened before. Many years ago, on one occasion, I was the only member present. N. I. BOWDITCH."

[FOOT-NOTE. It had happened once before [October 7, 1836], and has happened once since. And there have been various occasions when only one Trustee was present; viz. June 14, 1835, Mr. Bond; January 5, 1836, Mr. Tuckerman; August 6, 1843, Mr. Andrews; August 6, 1847, Mr. Hooper, &c. &c.]

November 18, 1849. Gas was ordered to be introduced into the Hospital, under the superintendence of Mr. Dexter.

October 11, 1850. Signor Antonio Sarti, a distinguished anatomist, and the proprietor of some very beautiful and expensive wax-preparations, who had recently been delivering public lectures, died at the Hospital, September 21. The Trustees, considering his services and labors in the cause of science, preferred to make no charge for his board while in the institution. The Chairman, accordingly, waited on Madame Sarti, and communicated to her this vote.

October 16, 1850. The subject of putting an appropriate inscription on the statue of Apollo, presented by Mr. Everett [1845], was referred to the Visiting Committee, with full powers.

November 9, 1850. The following preamble and vote, as prepared by the Chairman, were adopted and recorded:

"A communication having been received from William Appleton, Esq., President of this Corporation, announcing his donation of twenty thousand dollars for the erection of buildings at the M'Lean Asylum for the Insane, designed especially for such patients as shall have previously dwelt in residences of a spacious and cheerful character, and with the view of affording, as far as possible, to this the wealthiest class of our inmates the accustomed comforts and conveniences of home,— voted that the Trustees gratefully accept this munificent gift.

They recognize in it the same practical wisdom and the same true benevolence that have heretofore furnished to this institution a fund of ten thousand dollars, the income of which is to be for ever applied in aid of our poorer patients. The enlarged philanthropy which has thus provided for the equal relief of *rich* and *poor*, when suffering under the greatest of human deprivations, will ever entitle Mr. Appleton to a high rank among the benefactors of this community."

January 22, 1851. A letter claiming compensation for a cow killed while boarded at the Asylum was referred to the Visiting Committee, *with full powers*.

John A. Lowell, Esq., having been for several months absent in Europe, and intending to remain absent all this year, the Board of Visitors elected in his stead Dr. William J. Dale to be a Trustee of the institution.

[Foot-Note. When Mr. Lowell shall have returned from his present tour, he will, on the occurrence of a vacancy, receive a cordial welcome from his old associates, should he be willing at a future day to resume his duties as a Trustee.]

It is believed that Dr. Dale is the first practising physician who has ever held a seat as Trustee; though Dr. Robbins had practised for several years, and B. D. Greene and Charles Amory, Esqs., had studied that profession.

March 2, 1851. In accepting a legacy of twenty thousand dollars from Dr. Charles W. Wilder, of Leominster, the Trustees " would notice two circumstances by which its value is especially enhanced. Large as it is in itself, the gift comes not, as might have been supposed, from one of the wealthiest of our own citizens, but has been contributed from the more moderate fortunes of one of our country-towns. It is believed to be the first and only bequest ever received by this institution from a member of that profession which, more than any other, is competent fully to appreciate the importance of this public charity, and to form an accurate opinion as to the judgment and fidelity with which its concerns have been administered. It is a gift, noble in itself; a gift from the country to the poor of the city, from a physician, in aid of the sick and suffering."

Twenty-five dollars was voted in aid of a patient who has become blind.

March 16, 1851. The Committee on naming the wards made a report, which was read and laid on the table for future consideration. It has not yet been accepted. It recommends the giving to the wards the names of those who have been the chief benefactors of the institution, either by donations or by professional services.

The Secretary was instructed to procure a record-book, in which to enter all past and future devises and bequests made to the institution, extracts from wills, &c.

March 30, 1851. It was voted that the Board sincerely regret the retirement of Dr. [George] Hayward from a situation [one of the Visiting Surgeons of the Hospital] which for twenty-five years he has filled with so much honor to himself, and usefulness to the community. It was his privilege to perform the first capital operation rendered painless by the influence of ether, thus connecting this institution with the establishment of the greatest discovery of the age.

April 16, 1851. "Owing to a storm so severe as to render it unsafe to cross the bridges, the usual quarterly meeting was not held to-day."

[FOOT-NOTE. It was in this storm that the light-house at Minot's Ledge was destroyed, and a steeple blown down in Charlestown.]

May 18, 1851. The Secretary laid before the Board the volume prepared by him, containing a record of all bequests to the institution. It is executed with great accuracy and elegance.

July 11, 1851. The Superintendent was "authorized to buy two dozen silver forks for use of the Hospital."

[NOTE. Pages 383 to 455 are devoted to statistics and anecdotes. On page 386 it is stated that, at the Asylum, "The last interview of Charles I. and his children, *in worsteds*, the handiwork and the gift of one of our patients, hangs beside the picture of John M'Lean."]

EXTRACTS WHICH FOLLOW ARE FROM A CONTINUA-
TION OF MR. BOWDITCH'S HISTORY BY THE
REV. DR. GEORGE E. ELLIS.

The report to the Trustees of the Hospital, made by the Committee for the year 1851, closes with the following acknowledgment of the labor of love and zeal done by Mr. Bowditch in behalf of the Institution, which he had served with such fidelity in very many ways: —

"Your Committee would also, among the important events of last year, notice the publication of a most valuable and interesting History of the Hospital, by the private liberality of the Chairman of this Board, who has for so many years aided the government of the Institution by his counsel and experience, and cheered its inmates by his kindness and encouraging sympathy."

November 2, 1851. The Physicians and Surgeons made a communication to the Board, which was referred for report to Messrs. Dale and Stevenson, relative to the appointment of a Chemist and Microscopist for the Hospital. November 16, the Committee on the appointment of a Chemist and Microscopist made a report, which was accepted; and the votes recommended by them were passed, — that such an officer should be elected annually by the Trustees, with the privilege, when matters of sufficient importance have accumulated as results, of publishing them to the world, under the patronage of the Hospital, and at the discretion of the Surgeons and Physicians.

November 30, 1851. Dr. Bell reported another of the cases occasionally arising at the Asylum, of a complaint on the part of a patient of alleged maltreatment, and requested the appointment of a committee to investigate the case. Messrs. Bowditch, Rogers, Lawrence, and Stevenson were accordingly appointed as such a committee. The matter is regarded as worthy of mention here only as it illustrates the care and patience and fidelity which have uniformly been engaged on the part of the Trustees in the thorough examination of every similar complaint brought against the officials in charge of either branch of this institution, or against any subordinate or attendant. As might be expected, the report of the Committee, made at the next meeting, December 14, asserted that, after the most minute and impartial investigation of the case, the charge alleged was wholly groundless. The Secretary was instructed to read this report to the attorneys of the complainant if they should be desirous of hearing it.

December 28, 1851. The Superintendent was directed, under the advice of the Chairman, to procure tablets to be placed on or under each of the portraits in the Hospital, each tablet to contain the name and date of the death of the original of the portrait. This direction was carried into effect in November of the next year.

May 7, 1852. A communication from the Physicians and Surgeons was laid before the Board, asking whether they should not return a negative answer to an inquiry made of them by the House Pupils, — "If they are to consider themselves amenable in matters purely medical and surgical to any officer of the Corporation, other than the attending Physicians and Surgeons?" The action of the Trustees, when this "inquiry" came before them, might well be inferred from their own sense of their duties, rights and responsibilities, from their ready and courteous recognition of the professional and official claims of those to whom they delegated authority within the walls of the Hospital, and from their intention to retain their own reserved authority, even if the assertion of it involved a rebuke to any who might bring it under question. It was —

Voted, "That every officer of the Hospital, in the discharge of his duties, is responsible to the Board of Trustees. In matters purely medical or surgical, indeed, the Board confide in the ability and discretion of gentlemen selected by themselves, and would not think of interfering with their prescriptions or practice. But should a specific charge be made against any Physician or Surgeon, either of a want of competency and skill, or of humanity or delicacy in the treatment of a patient, the Trustees would feel it to be not only their right, but their duty, to investigate the circumstances of the case, and to act as in their opinion should be required by a due regard to the interests of the Institution and of the community. So likewise the Trustees will not interfere with the professional duties prescribed to medical and surgical pupils by their immediate superiors, but will, nevertheless, at all times, hold them accountable for the performance of those duties in an exact, kind, and proper manner."

"*Voted*, That the Trustees cannot refrain from expressing their surprise at the inquiry thus submitted by the medical and surgical pupils, — an inquiry which would seem to be founded on an entire misapprehension of their own true position, and an unwillingness to recognize the paramount authority of this Board, or of its duly constituted committees."

A copy of the foregoing votes was ordered to be sent to each of the Physicians and Surgeons, and a Committee of the Trustees was instructed "to inquire whether there has been any want of due subordination and propriety on the part of any of the House Pupils," and especially to investigate the circumstances of a case which had been brought to the notice of the Visiting Committee. The same Committee was to consider and report whether it was expedient to make any change in the rules and regulations in regard to House Pupils. As was to be expected, frankness and a mutual understanding disposed of this question.

June 7, 1852. Up to this time, the semi-monthly meetings of the Trustees had been held at the Hospital, after the close of the second service on Sunday. The meeting on Monday, June 7, 1852, was held at the American Insurance Office, in State Street, as were also several subsequent meetings.

November 21, 1852. Action was taken on an occasion the occurrence of which was the cause of painful interest within the walls of the Hospital and to the community outside of it. At the meeting of the Board on November 7, the case of James Clancey, who had died on that day in the Hospital, had been referred for full investigation and report to a special Committee. The report, which was submitted at a meeting on November 10, and then laid upon the table for future consideration, was acted upon at a meeting on November 15, and, after being amended, was unanimously accepted, and ordered to be recorded at this meeting, on the 21st. It appeared from the report, after a most thorough investigation, that by a mistake which had occurred, without, however, involving any culpable neglect on the part of the Hospital Apothecary, the Surgeons accidentally administered chloroform for the usual preparation of chloric ether, to three subjects of operations. The third of these patients, James Clancey, whose arm had been amputated, after the use of the anæsthetic, sunk into a state of insensibility, from which he recovered only to die in a few hours afterwards; and also, that when he was apparently in a dying condition, one of the Surgeons "accidentally poured into his mouth a quantity of undiluted caustic ammonia."

The Committee considered the circumstances as disclosed to be of a very serious character. After a very full discussion, the Board, "having good reason to believe that every precaution will be taken to prevent such deplorable accidents in future," voted, "That no further action be had in the premises." Also voted, "That this event is a solemn warning to all persons connected with the Hospital to exercise the greatest care in the performance of the delicate and difficult duties which devolve upon them."

January 19, 1853. The Trustees received a letter of that date from Dr. John C. Warren, requesting that his name be not included among the candidates at their next election. The preamble and vote which were thereupon passed by the Trustees must be copied here, alike on the score of their historical as of their personal character: —

"More than forty years ago Dr. Warren, and his associate, Dr. James Jackson, by an admirable circular letter, first called the attention of the public to the necessity of a Hospital. Becoming thus one of our original founders, he was appointed our first Surgeon, and has been annually re-elected to that office ever since.

"His name has become illustrious in the annals of American Surgery, and reflects honor on the Institution which is so deeply indebted to him for its establishment and success. Finding here those opportunities of professional practice by which his own skill and experience were from year to year increased, he has, in return, devoted to the gratuitous performance of his official duties among us much time and thought during a long life. By pecuniary donations and otherwise, he has manifested a continued interest in the welfare of the Hospital. And now that, having completed his labors, he is about to retire from this honorable and responsible situation, the Trustees would assure him of their best wishes for his future health and happiness. And they would congratulate the Institution and himself on the circumstance that he leaves behind him in our service, and, as we hope, for many years to come, a son whose high professional skill and attainments are universally recognized as worthy of his parentage.

" *Voted*, That Dr. Warren be requested to sit for his bust or portrait, to be preserved at the Hospital, and that Messrs. Lowell and Dexter be a committee to communicate to him this wish of the Trustees.

February 6, 1853. The Chairman was "requested to collect, if possible, a complete set of the reports and other documents of the Hospital, and to have them bound and placed in the library." Mr. Bowditch had already earnestly devoted his researches to that object; and the Trustees committed the matter to one most willing and competent to effect it.

March 20, the Chairman, Mr. Bowditch, received the thanks of the Board for the bound volumes of reports and other Hospital documents, which he presented at this meeting.

February 20, 1853. A letter was received from Homer Goodhue, resigning the office of male Supervisor at the Asylum. In accepting his resignation, the Trustees instructed the Visiting Committee to express "their regret at parting with one who had so long and faithfully performed the responsible duties of his office, and to request his acceptance of a gold watch, with a suitable inscription upon its case, as a testimonial of their appreciation of his services."

February 5, 1854. The Chairman in a letter to the Board communicated memoranda, which he had made and gathered in preparing matter for the tablets under the portraits, — of the dates of the birth and death of the benefactors of the Hospital. These memoranda are entered upon the records.

February 19, 1854. The Visiting Committee presented a surgical operating chair invented by Dr. Henry J. Bigelow, and constructed under his supervision; and it was voted, "That in consideration of the excellence of the chair, and the ingenuity displayed by Dr. Bigelow in its construction, it be called 'The Bigelow Operating Chair,' in honor of the inventor.''

March 19, 1854. The Trustees, at their meeting, received a communication from the executors of the late Judah Touro, of New Orleans, announcing a legacy in his will of $10,000 to the Hospital; whereupon the following preamble and vote were unanimously adopted: —

"More than thirty years ago there died in this city one, of Jewish faith and parentage, who bequeathed to this institution the sum of $10,000. The name of [Abraham] Touro has thenceforth been familiar to us as that of one of our chief benefactors. And now another of the same name and lineage, an eminent merchant, who for fifty years has resided in the distant city of New Orleans, has, by like liberal bequests, remembered the home of his own youth and its various charitable institutions which were the objects of his brother's bounty: therefore —

Voted, That the Trustees, in accepting the legacy of the late Judah Touro, recognize in it an act prompted by fraternal love and a philanthropy not confined within the narrow bounds of time, place, or sect."

After the subject had frequently been before the Board at its meetings, a Committee to whom it had been referred reported at this meeting in favor of erecting a building for patients suffering under offensive diseases, near the north-west corner of the Hospital grounds, at a cost of about $10,000. A remonstrance against said location from those residing near the Hospital was read; and it was voted that Messrs. Bullard, Rogers, and Wigglesworth be a Building Committee to erect a building according to the report of the said Committee.

November 5, 1854. The Physicians and Surgeons offered a communication to the Board recommending the establishment of a Pathological Museum at the Hospital, and the Visiting Committee were instructed to report upon the subject. November 19, the Visiting Committee reported that it was expedient to establish a Pathological Museum at the Hospital. Whereupon it was "voted that the report be accepted, and that the subject be referred back to the Committee to report a system of rules for the management of the Museum, and to nominate a suitable person as Curator."

December 3, 1854. A report from the Visiting Committee on a Pathological Cabinet was accepted, with its recommendations, which were as follows: that $100 be appropriated for commencing such a cabinet; that a Curator for it should be chosen annually by the Trustees; that it should be his duty to preserve morbid specimens and arrange them in the way best fitted to make them useful; and that he should make all the autopsies excepting such as shall be made by the attending Physicians and Surgeons, and shall observe all the regulations now in force or that may be made respecting them. Upon the nomination of the same Committee, the Board then elected Dr. Calvin Ellis Curator of the Pathological Cabinet.

February 4, 1855. In the annual report for 1854, it is stated that the urgent need that had long been felt of a separate ward for cases of a foul and dangerous nature, to relieve and secure other patients from discomfort and risk, had during the year been supplied. At the cost of $12,000, including that for a necessary sea-wall, a commodious building of two stories ["the Brick," 1899], west of the main edifice, had been erected, containing sixteen rooms, with every needful convenience.

Attention is called to the dilapitated state of the fence, and the opportunity for embellishing and improving by walks, shrubbery, flowers and culture, the extensive grounds of the Hospital, reaching as they do to low-water mark.

March 18, 1855. The Visiting Committee reported on a communication received from Dr. Bacon, and referred to them, that the duties of a Microscopist more appropriately belong to the office of Curator of the Pathological Cabinet, and advised that hereafter the said duties should be performed by that officer instead of by Dr. Bacon who shall remain Chemist. The report was accepted.

August 15, 1855. The report of the Committee on the resignation of Dr. [Jacob] Bigelow ends as follows: —

"And the Committee recommend that he be requested by the Trustees to permit his bust or portrait to be taken by a competent artist, to be preserved in the Hospital."

In accepting this report, the Board authorized and instructed the same Committee to take the necessary steps for carrying their recommendation into effect.

Sept. 15, 1855. A Committee, to whom had been referred the converting of the Lecture and Reception Room in the Hospital into rooms for patients, reported to the Board that they had attended to that duty, and that, through the changes they had made, the number of beds for patients had been increased by twenty-three, at an expense, including the furniture, of $3,009.45. The new wards thus formed were appropriated to male patients.

October 12, 1855. A special Committee was empowered to contract for a new fence around the grounds of the Hospital, at an expense not exceeding $5,500.

February 3, 1856. In the Annual Report for 1855, it is stated that "the average length of time of the stay of free patients, which in 1853 had been seven weeks, had grown, in 1855, to eleven weeks and four days." [NOTE. The fact that the average time of paying and free patients during 1898 was *eighteen days*, is a strong proof of the beneficent results attained by modern medical and surgical practice.]

Dr. Bell, in his 1855 report, mentions the fact that at the Asylum "The experiment of permitting the intermingling of the sexes in daily religious exercises and in occasions of festivity, though under the close supervision of officers and attendants, was thoroughly tested for several years, but its inconveniences long ago led to its abandonment."

March 16, 1856. Mr. G. H. Shaw, for the Committee on a new fence around the Hospital grounds, reported that he had procured subscriptions to the amount of $3,250 for that object, made on the condition that enough to cover the expense should yet be obtained. It was then "voted that the Chairman of the Board be authorized to subscribe, in behalf of the Trustees," the needful balance.

A Committee appointed upon the subject of the resignation of Dr. Bell were authorized to procure a bust or portrait of him to be placed in the Asylum.

February 22, 1857. Messrs. Stevenson and Lowell, to whom, at a previous meeting, had been referred a proposition that the Trustees, in behalf of the Hospital, should subscribe $1,000 to the fund then solicited from the public at large in behalf of Dr. W. T. G. Morton, for his discovery and use of an anæsthetic, after a lucid report recommended the following vote, which with the report, was unanimously approved by the Trustees : —

Voted, That the Chairman of this Board be requested to subscribe, on behalf of the Massachusetts General Hospital, one thousand dollars towards the fund which it is proposed to establish for the benefit of Dr. W. T. G. Morton, as a memorial of the great service which that gentleman has rendered to science and humanity, in connection with the discovery of the uses of ether.

March 8, 1857. Messrs. Rogers and Stevenson were appointed a Committee to procure a bust or portrait of Dr. George Hayward for the Hospital.

April 10, 1857. A committee recommended the establishment of the office of Artist of the Hospital. The Board approving, it was —

Voted, That the said office be hereby established, and the following rules and regulations be adopted : —

"'ARTIST OF THE HOSPITAL.

"'ART. 1. He shall, under the direction and at the discretion of the Physicians and Surgeons, make accurate drawings of such anomalous and rare cases of disease as shall be useful for future reference and examination.

"'ART. 2. He shall be present and assist the Physicians and Surgeons whenever his services may be desirable.

"'ART. 3. All copies and drawings shall be carefully preserved in a portfolio provided for the purpose, and shall be placed in the Pathological Cabinet, under the care of the Curator; and they shall not be taken from the Hospital without the consent of the Visiting Committee."

November 22, 1857. An application having been received at the meeting on November 8, and then laid on the table, from Sarah W. Salisbury, "a graduate of the Female Medical College, to be admitted for the purpose of obtaining practical knowledge in some of the branches of Medical Science,"— it was at this meeting taken from the table, when it was —

Voted, That the Secretary communicate to Miss Salisbury a copy of the rules and regulations of the Hospital, and inform her that the Trustees deem any departure from the rules and regulations to be inexpedient.

March 21, 1858. The Board accepted the devises and bequests made to the Corporation in trust in the will of the late John G. Treadwell [Donor of $43,703.91]; and instructed the Treasurer to keep two accounts of the property thus received: one account to be credited with the sum of five thousand dollars, to be designated, "The Treadwell Library Fund, in trust"; and the other account, credited with the balance, to be designated "The Treadwell Fund, in trust." It was also voted that Messrs. Rogers, Lamb, and Mason "be a

Committee to take charge of the Medical Library bequeathed to the Corporation by the late John G. Treadwell."

Harvard College had declined the bequest proffered to them in the will of Dr. Treadwell, because of "unusual and embarrassing conditions attached to it."

March 31, 1858. On the report and recommendation of a Committee appointed on December 20, 1857, to examine into the internal affairs of the Hospital, it was "voted that in the opinion of this Board it is expedient to establish the office of Resident Physician at the Hospital, with powers and duties hereafter to be prescribed."

April 27, 1858. The Board directed the Committee on the Treadwell bequest to adapt the room then occupied by the Physicians and Surgeons to the reception of the Treadwell Library.

May 23, 1858. Dr. Benjamin Shurtleff Shaw was by ballot elected Resident Physician, and Dr. Samuel L. Abbott Physician to out-door patients at the Hospital, in conformity with the new arrangement of offices and distribution of duties which had been approved by recommendation of the Committee on the Internal Administration of the Hospital.

June 16, 1858. Miss Sarah W. Salisbury, by letter, renewed her urgent application for admission to the Hospital for the purpose before stated. [*Vide* Nov. 22, 1857.] The Trustees directed the Secretary to inform her that there had been no change in the views of the Trustees since the reply to her former application. The previous resignation of Capt. Girdler was then acted upon and accepted, and it was "voted that the thanks of Board be tendered to Capt. Girdler for his long and faithful services as Superintendent of the Hospital, and that in consideration thereof the Treasurer be directed to pay him his regular salary to October next."

September 14, 1858. The Board authorized the Superintendent of the Asylum to expend one hundred dollars for books for the use of patients, and to make such arrangements for amusements for them as he may deem expedient, all under the supervision of the Chairman of the Board.

December 19, 1858. A claim had been advanced by Mrs. Lydia N. Raymond to an interest in the house, No. 26 Beacon Street, then in possession of the Hospital, under the will of the late M. P. Sawyer. Mr. Rogers, in behalf of a Committee to which the matter had been referred, submitted a report upon it, with votes, which were accepted by the Board, as follows: —

"*Voted*, That in consideration of the doubt which exists as to the testamentary intentions of Matthias P. Sawyer, deceased, respecting the estate numbered 26 Beacon Street, now in the lawful possession of this Corporation, by virtue of the residuary clause of his will, and of the handsome sums of money which they have received, and still expect to receive from his benevolent disposition towards them, this Corporation hereby surrenders their legal rights in this estate, and relinquishes the same to Mrs. Raymond."

January 19, 1859. Authority was given to the Chairman of the Board to execute an indenture in behalf of the Corporation with the City of Boston, providing for the filling up of the flats lying between the Hospital grounds and the Harbor Commissioners' line.

February 27, 1859. The Board voted "that three hundred dollars per annum be placed at the disposal of the Superintendent and Physician of the Asylum to be used in the purchase of books for the permanent increase of the library."

November 6, 1859. The Board voted an amendment of a rule of the Hospital, so that it should read, "any individual on the payment of one hundred dollars shall be entitled to a free bed at the Hospital for one year."

On a report from Mr. Rogers it was "voted that this Board deem the practice of admitting inebriates into the Asylum to be highly prejudicial to its best interests, and that hereafter no such persons be admitted as patients without the express order of the Board in each case."

January 25, 1860. The thanks of the Board were voted to the family of the late Dr. Perry for a photograph likeness of him, received from the hands of Dr. Bowditch.

February 5, 1860. In their Annual Report for 1859 the Trustees say: "The object of the Hospital being to afford substantial relief to the largest possible number of persons, it is not consistent with it to use even beds temporarily unoccupied for patients with incurable diseases. It is more in conformity with the design of the institution that eight or ten sufferers by acute disease should be successively relieved, than that the bed which they might occupy should be used, it may be for a year, by a chronic incurable."

Dr. Tyler in his annual report for 1859 states that " Many patients have attended concerts and lectures in Boston, and public worship on Sunday in various churches. Every Sunday evening a sermon is read, with singing, in one of the wings."

The Trustees instructed the Secretary to inform the Treasurer that it would be agreeable to them to have him participate freely in their discussions whenever he should attend the meetings.

February 19, 1860. The Chairman from a Committee reported, recommending the appointing a "Standing Committee on Alterations and Repairs" at the Hospital and Asylum, with full powers in all cases in which the expense would not exceed one hundred dollars, the consent of the Board being requisite for any proposed outlay beyond that amount. The report and its recommendations were approved. The rules and regulations were amended according to these new provisions, and the new Committee was appointed for the current year.

June 19, 1860. Permission was granted to the House Pupils to sleep and take their breakfasts at the Hospital until otherwise ordered.

July 3, 1860. During a contemplated absence of Mr. Rogers, Mr. Wigglesworth was chosen temporary Chairman of the Board.

October 12, 1860. The Board voted "that in consideration of the advanced age of Miss Taylor, and her long and faithful services as nurse, which are held in grateful remembrance by the Trustees, she be relieved from all duties at the Hospital, and that her wages be continued till further order of the Board." In their Annual Report for this year, the Trustees mention the fact that Miss Rebecca Taylor "has efficiently and faithfully performed the duties of nurse in the Hospital for thirty-four years, and to more than four thousand persons."

February 10, 1861. Mrs. Sarah L. Gallison having resigned the office of Matron of the Hospital, her resignation was accepted, with a continuation of her salary through the current quarter.

January 23, 1861. The report for the previous year, 1860, is very elaborate, and contains matter of much interest. In addition to other general funds, there had been an extra dividend of $15,000 from the Hospital Life Insurance Company, without which there would have been a great deficiency of means. The Corporation had, up to this time, received from that insurance company since its establishment, according to the provisions of its charter, $231,687.50, being "the most munificent of all its munificent benefactors."

Dr. Tyler, in his annual report, remarks that "Fidelity and kindness are the laws of the house. Patients taken away *uncured*, and employés discharged for unfitness, are the sources of all the malign reports about a well-ordered Asylum. Those who are *thoroughly recovered* are always enthusiasts in their praise and gratitude. An *early* resort to the Asylum in *every* case of insanity, and a patient delay till the cure is thorough and confirmed, before removal, are the prime conditions of benefit."

April 17, 1861. The death of Mr. Nathaniel I. Bowditch, Vice-President of the Corporation, was announced. [NOTE. Pages 561 to 570 (inclusive) are devoted to his memory. A foot-note to page 569 reads: "There is an excellent likeness, in pho ograph, of Mr. Bowditch in the Trustees' room at the Hospital, the gift of Mrs. Bowditch."]

May 5, 1861. The Board were informed by the Treasurer that the late Mr. Bowditch had in his will bequeathed to the Hospital $5,000 to constitute a "Wooden-leg Fund," and $2,000 as a fund for the republication of the History of the Hospital.

At the same meeting, the Secretary was directed to communicate to his Excellency Governor Andrew the following vote, passed in view of the pending civil war: — "That the Trustees of the Massachusetts General Hospital assure the Executive of the Commonwealth that, in the event of any diseased or wounded soldiers being returned to this city, they shall consider it their duty and privilege to extend to them all the succor and relief that may be within their power."

August 27, 1861. The House Pupils having petitioned for leave to board in the Hospital, the Trustees, by vote, granted permission until further order.

September 10, 1861. Mr. R. M. Mason resigned his place on the Board on account of intended absence abroad.

November 17, 1861. The Chairman, Mr. Rogers, having previously announced to the Board that he would be unavoidably absent from Boston during much of the coming season, in attendance at Washington as a member of the National Sanitary Commission, the Board elected Mr. Bullard as Chairman *pro tem.*, while Mr. Rogers should be absent.

February 5, 1862. Dr. Shaw, in the Annual Report for 1861, repeats his suggestions as to the intent of the Hospital for the treatment of curable patients, rather than for an Infirmary, and refers to the proposed City Hospital as designed to receive contagious and incurable cases.

February 24, 1862. Mr. H. B. Rogers, then absent at Washington, was re-elected Chairman, Mr. Bullard being chosen to fill the place temporarily.

It was —"*Voted*, That the subject of proper accommodations in this Hospital for the sick and wounded of the United States army be referred to Drs. Dale and Howe, to consider and report to this Board at an early meeting; and in the meantime that Dr. Dale shall have authority to place for treatment in the Hospital any invalid soldier for whom there is suitable room, the rate of their board being $4.50 per week."

Dr. Dale reported at the next meeting, March 23, — " That, unless some extraordinary exigency should occur, the accommodations now afforded by this Institution are ample for the present."

A communication from the Custom-house Collector of Boston was received, enclosing a copy of an inquiry from the Treasury Department at Washington, relative to obtaining contract proposals from public and private hospitals, for the accommodation of sick seamen. Whereupon it was — "*Voted*, That the Resident Physician be directed to reply to the Collector, that, whilst the Trustees would be glad to receive all patients for whom there is room in the Hospital, the organization and rules of the Institution and its relation to the City and State are such as to prevent any contract undertaking of the kind desired."

May 4, 1862. Miss Susan L. Kilborn made a communication to the Trustees, asking leave to visit the Hospital. The communication was laid on the table.

October 10, 1862. A communication from Dr. Shaw [Resident Physician at the Hospital] was laid before the Trustees, relative to a request of the United States Sanitary Commission that he would act on a Board of Special Inspection of General Hospitals of the army, requiring a service for two terms, of two weeks each, during the next six months. It was then "voted that leave of absence be granted to Dr. Shaw for the time and purpose named, provided he makes such arrangement for supplying his place during his absence as shall be satisfactory to the Chairman of this Board."

The same leave was granted by the Board to Dr. Tyler, on October 15, for the same purpose and on the same conditions.

November 2, 1862. Mr. Bullard, for a Committee, reported that a marble bust of the late William Appleton [President of the Corporation and Donor of $40,000] had been procured and placed in the Trustees' room at the Asylum.

February 4, 1863. Dr. Howe and Mr. Lowell were appointed a Committee, "to look after the interests of this institution in the proposed legislation on the Subject of Asylums for the Insane, now pending before the Legislature of this State."

February 15, 1863. A communication was read from Dr. Solomon D. Townsend, declining to be re-elected one of the Visiting Surgeons of the Hospital. It was "*Resolved*, That Dr. Townsend be requested to sit for his portrait or bust."

March 15, 1863. Leave was granted to Dr. Shaw to accept the appointment of Commissioner, or Examining Surgeon, under the authority of the United States Pension Office, — his services to be rendered at the Hospital. This office was to be held by him in accordance with documents communicated to the Board relative thereto.

March 29, 1863. By request of the Visiting Physicians, the Board made a change in the regulations, which allowed Dr. Ellis, the Microscopist and Curator of the Pathological Cabinet, to perform their duties in case of their necessary absence.

May 3, 1863. Permission was granted by the Board to Messrs. C. Tyler and J. M. Pinkerton, executors of the late Dr. Bell, to take his portrait from the Asylum that an engraving might be made from it. In terminating the connection which Mr. and Mrs. Columbus Tyler had so long held, as Steward and Matron at the M'Lean Asylum, the Trustees voted that their salaries should be paid to the 1st of July ensuing.

May 17, 1863. Mr. Rogers, for a Committee that had been appointed to endeavor to obtain a reduction of the charge for water, reported that they had had a full hearing before the Board of Aldermen, who had rejected the petition for a reduction of the rates, upon legal grounds, stated in City Document No. 47, for 1863.

January 20, 1864. A question having arisen as to the use of the surplus income of Mr. Bowditch's Wooden-leg Fund, a Committee appointed for that purpose reported that the representatives of the family of the donor objected to any diversion of the income from the object specified by him.

February 28, 1864. "*Voted*, That a Surgeon to out-patients be and hereby is established, whose duties shall correspond generally with those of the Physician to the same department."

October 19, 1864. It was voted to hold the regular meetings of the Board henceforward on Friday instead of, as heretofore, on Sunday.

July 20, 1865. It was voted "that the Physicians and Surgeons to out-patients be authorized to charge such fees for their first visits as they may think proper, whenever they are satisfied of the ability of patients to pay the same."

October 2, 1865. It was voted that the quarterly meetings of the Board at the Asylum be henceforth held on the Fridays after the third Wednesdays of January, April, July, and October.

January 19, 1866. Mr. Bullard communicated the offer of Mr. Nathaniel Thayer of a donation of the sum of twenty-five thousand dollars to the Corporation, provided that seventy-five thousand more were raised. [The result of this offer was a prompt subscription of $100,800 by ninety-eight persons.]

June 29, 1866. A report and plans were submitted for alterations and improvements in the surgical operating theatre; and Dr. H. J. Bigelow appeared to urge their adoption. The subject was recommitted for further details on July 13. Progress was announced, on November 2, in the plans for a new surgical theatre.

January 11, 1867. Dr. Tyler wrote to the Board stating his need of relaxation from his cares, and his desire for leave of absence for six months. The Board voted an expression of sympathy for him, and in consideration of the value of his services gave him leave of absence for a year, with a continuation of his salary.

March 27, 1867. The Board voted "that it is expedient to erect on the Hospital grounds, a building for surgical operations, and for the accommodation of out-door patients; and that the plans and estimates for such a building, presented to the Board, be adopted." Messrs. Rogers, Bullard, and Storrow were appointed a Building Committee, with full power in the case, the expense not to exceed fifty thousand dollars.

April 19, 1867. A proposition had been suggested to charge medical students a fee for admissions to the lectures and operations at the Hospital. A report of a Committee, which thought it inexpedient to do this, was approved by the Board.

May 17, 1867. Messrs. Beebe, Bullard, and Eliot were instructed to consider and report upon the subject of religious services at the Asylum.

June 28, 1867. At the meeting of the Board on May 17, a letter, from Hon. Charles G. Loring had been read, recommending the admission of Miss Sophia Blake to "the medical visitations at the Hospital"; also a note from Miss Blake and Susan Dimmock, asking leave to share the educational advantages of the Hospital, especially in the female wards. The subject had been referred to the Visiting Committee, with the addition of Mr. Eliot, whose report, recommending the passage of the three following resolutions, was adopted by the Board, on June 28 : —

"1. That Chap. III., Art. 3, of the Rules and Regulations for the Hospital, may be so interpreted as to include female as well as male students.

2. That the admission of female students be left to the discretion of the Visiting Physicians and Surgeons, individually.

3. That female students, whenever admitted, shall be placed in classes separate from male students, and shall attend the clinical practice of the female wards exclusively."

September 27, 1867. The Massachusetts Board of State Charities, having required a report from this Corporation, under chapter 243 of the Acts of 1867, the Secretary stated "that he had in reply informed the Board of State Charities that this Corporation would make no report unless further called upon, on the ground that this Corporation is not a State Charity within the meaning of the statute."

October 18, 1867. Dr. J. Collins Warren, in a letter acknowledging the receipt of the resolutions passed by the Board on the death of his late father [Dr. J. Mason Warren], informed the Board of a legacy under his father's will, to the Trustees, of $2000, to be called the "Warren Prize Fund" [in memory of his father, Dr. John C. Warren, the interest of which, every three years, is to be awarded for the best dissertation considered worthy of a premium, on some subject in physiology, surgery, or pathological anatomy].

Mr. Eliot, for a Committee, offered the following preamble and resolutions: —

"The death of Dr. James Jackson, one of the founders of the Massachusetts General Hospital and its first Physician, whose active service extended from April 6, 1817, to October 13, 1837, and who, as Consulting Physician, was connected with the Institution to the close of his earthly life, August 27, 1867, is an event of so singular and so affecting an interest to the Hospital, that the Trustees have delayed noticing it officially until a quarterly meeting should draw them together in full numbers. They can add nothing to his well-deserved reputation, but they perform an act of simple duty in offering a sincere and grateful tribute to his honored memory.

"*Resolved*, That the Trustees of the Massachusetts General Hospital recall, with deep sensibility, Dr. Jackson's long connection with the Institution, which he was prominent in founding and extending, and to which, while he retained his powers, he gave the great benefit of his name, his science, his advice, and his influence.

"*Resolved*, That his remarkable traits as a Physician, well known and appreciated before the Hospital was founded, and fully acknowledged during the half-century of its existence, have been of inestimable value to its administration not only during the term of his attendance in our wards, but in the subsequent period, during which his counsel and support, while he could give them, have never failed our predecessors or ourselves.

"*Resolved*, That his personal as well as his professional qualities, his activity without imprudence, his decision without dogmatism, his dignity that never wounded, his conscientiousness that never provoked, his exhaustless sympathies, which made him the brother or the father, as well as the physician of those to whom he ministered, bearing their troubles as his own, and alleviating by the charm of his presence the pains which he could not remove by his skill, his unwearied study, his fruitful knowledge, his contributions to the science and literature of medicine, and his relations to the elder and younger members of the profession, gave him a position at the Hospital as exclusively his own as that which he held in the community.

"*Resolved*, That his labors, as efficient as they were devoted, and his counsels, as wise as they were earnest, rendering him both the ornament and the safeguard of the Hospital, are among its most precious traditions, and that they are to be cherished for the sake not merely of its past history, which they had so large a share in forming, but of its future course, to which, if they are faithfully preserved, they will be helpful guides.

"*Resolved*, That the Trustees remove his name from the list of their living associates, only to place it, where it belongs, at the head of the departed benefactors of the Hospital. And to the end that his memory may continue among us, as we think he would have best preferred it to continue, the free bed which was placed in 1837 at his disposal for life shall remain the Jackson Free Bed, perpetuating his attachment to the Hospital, and his benevolence to humanity."

These resolutions having been unanimously adopted, the Secretary was directed to communicate them to the family, and to furnish a copy to the public press.

Mr. F. H. Jackson, son of Dr. Jackson, communicated to the Board a bequest from his late father to the Hospital, of a portrait of M. Louis, of Paris. The same was gratefully accepted, and placed upon the walls of the Hospital.

The portrait was a gift from M. Louis, in 1833, to a son of Dr. Jackson, who had died in early manhood. Dr. Jackson "valued this picture more highly than anything that he owned." When M. Louis heard what disposition had been made of it " he expressed himself as highly pleased."

November 15, 1867. Mr. Beebe, for a Committee that had been appointed in May, upon the subject of religious services at the Asylum, made a report, on which the Board resolved that it is expedient to establish such services; that they should be wholly free from a sectarian character; that the Committee procure plans and estimates for a chapel at the Asylum, the present hall to be in the meanwhile used for the purpose; and that the Committee consult with the Superintendent with regard to a chaplain *pro tem.*, and for a suitable incumbent of the office.

January 17, 1868. The nomination by the Committee of Rev. David G. Haskins, to the office of Chaplain, *pro tem.*, at the Asylum, was confirmed.

February 21, 1868. The salary of the Treasurer was increased to $1000.

April 17, 1868. Permission was granted, on request, to the Massachusetts Medical Society to hold their annual meeting in June in the operating theatre of the Hospital.

April 24, 1868. The salary of the Chaplain at the Asylum was fixed at $1000.

July 31, 1868. A faithful attendant on the kitchen of the Asylum, on leaving after twenty-five years of service, received a present of one hundred dollars, with an appreciative letter of thanks.

February 3, 1869. In the Report for 1868, it is stated that a Dental Service had been added during the year, in connection with the Dental School of Harvard College, 1,078 persons having received its services.

Dr. Shaw, the Resident Physician, refers to religious services held for convalescents at the Hospital; and Dr. Tyler remarks that about a third of the patients at the Asylum have attended religious services in the hall on Sunday afternoons, receiving thus an influence evidently soothing and beneficial.

March 19, 1869. The Trustees voted that the Resident Physician be requested to prepare for publication a simple statement, that children have long been, and will continue to be, received and properly cared for at the Hospital.

June 4, 1869. After the Board had for some time had under consideration the appointment of two or more ladies to serve as visitors to the female wards of the Hospital, the measure was approved. Four ladies were elected by ballot to that service, and a Committee was appointed to confer with them on their proposed duties.

January 21, 1870. A Committee, to whom had been referred a circular addressed to the Trustees asking a contribution to a fund to be raised for the benefit of the family of the late Dr. Morton, and to pay for a monument to be erected over his remains, reported a form of reply to be sent by the Secretary, which was adopted, as follows:—

"The Trustees beg to say, that, while they are deeply sensible of the great blessing Dr. Morton conferred on mankind by proving that sulphuric ether can safely be used to produce insensibility to pain, even under the most serious surgical operations, they nevertheless feel that the appropriation of any portion of the funds of the Hospital for the purposes named in the circular would not be consistent with the uses for which they have been bestowed."

February 2, 1870. Dr. Tyler reports that there had been under treatment, at the Asylum [during 1869] 284 patients, of whom 184 remained. He regards the cases of insanity most proper for his Institution to be the violent and dangerous, and also the recent and curable. The soundness of the general principles of treatment adopted there is year by year verified. The study of French has been introduced with marked success into the Asylum, Madame Harney attending weekly upon separate classes of either sex. Mrs. Bunker, on another day, has classes in drawing. Mr. Moorhouse presides over an orchestra of twelve or fifteen male patients, one of the Trustees having generously given instruments for the purpose.

A "singing-school" under Mr. Hadley has united both sexes. These exercises have varied the inevitable monotony and cheered the weariness of life within the walls. Flowerbeds, garden grounds, chickens and ducks, embroidery, needlework for the poor, the carpenter's shop, concerts, readings, dancing parties [billiards and bowling], excursions in the harbor, festivals, wax works, and observance of holidays, have furnished their resources. More rooms like those in the Appleton wards are very much needed, as also an amusement hall, and a chapel. The religious services, under Rev. D. G. Haskins, are greatly prized; their omission for a single Sunday having been much mourned.

March 18, 1870. Six young ladies were appointed as assistant visitors to the female wards of the Hospital; viz., Miss Mary I. Bowditch, Miss Henrietta Townsend, Miss Helen A. Perkins, Mrs. Otto Cüntz, Miss Annie Putnam, and Miss Caroline Young. The sum of two hundred dollars was, on April 15, placed at the disposal of the lady visitors of the Hospital for procuring pictures to be hung upon the walls of the wards. On June 3, the lady visitors of the Hospital were authorized to visit the male wards also, at their discretion.

April 1, 1870. A communication was received from Dr. J. C. White, resigning the office of Visiting Physician of the Hospital, and asking to be appointed Physician to a department for skin diseases, which he recommends to be established at the Hospital. The communication was referred to Messrs. Rogers and Bullard for consideration and report. On May 6, a conference was asked for with the Visiting Physicians and Surgeons, by the Trustees, or a communication in any other form,' on the subject of the proposed department for skin diseases.

July 15, 1870. The attention of the officers of the Hospital was called to the rules relating to autopsies; and it was voted that a "Post-mortem Register" be kept to meet the requirements of those rules, — each entry in which shall be examined and signed by the Visiting Committee, — the book to be laid before the Trustees at their regular meetings. The Resident Physician was requested to keep a press copy of his official correspondence, including notices to relatives and friends of peceased patients.

Mr. Dalton made a communication from Dr. Henry J. Bigelow, presenting to the Hospital "a collection of instruments lately procured by him abroad, which are now placed in new cases in the operating theatre, at an aggregate cost of about three thousand two hundred and fifty dollars," also giving "the further sums of one thousand dollars, and of five hundred dollars, the income of the former to be used exclusively for the purchase of surgical instruments required by the attending surgeons, not including 'apparatus,' splints, nor general appliances, — and the latter sum to be devoted to the maintenance of a free bed for five years." It was voted that these very valuable gifts be accepted with gratitude.

On September 2, the Treasurer announced that he had received from Dr. Henry J. Bigelow an additional sum of seventeen hundred and fifty dollars, making the whole amount of his donation six thousand dollars. It was thereupon voted, —

"That the Treasurer be directed to establish the Henry J. Bigelow Fund in the sum of $1,750, of the principal of which

one hundred dollars *per annum*, for five years, shall be appropriated for Dr. Bigelow's free bed, and the income of which shal be applied annually to the purchase of surgical instruments, as may be agreed upon by the Surgeons and Trustees."
[NOTE. These statements with reference to Dr. Bigelow's gifts are inconsistent. The facts are, doubtless, that he gave instruments worth $3250 and $1750 in cash, making the whole amount of his donation $5000 — not $6000 or $6500 as shown, respectively, by the statement and the figures of the Treasurer. Of the cash, the sum of $500 was expended for a free bed for five years; and the remainder appears in the Treasurer's Report for 1898 as "Surgical Instrument Fund, a donation from Dr. H. J. Bigelow, $1250."]

October 21, 1870. After the Board had given a full and deliberate consideration to the subject, with the help of a Committee and a knowledge of the views of Dr. Shaw [Resident Physician] and of the Medical and Surgical officers, it was voted to establish a separate ward for the treatment of patients with skin diseases, and to appoint Dr. [J. C.] White as Physician to that department; it being understood that the measure was but an experiment, and the appointment but temporary.

February 1, 1871. The Treasurer's report for 1870 shows that the dividends, interest, and rent amounted to $38,334.18, being 7.70 *per cent* on the investments.

March 3, 1871. Mr. Dalton was requested to consider and report upon the subject of a yearly publication of important medical and surgical cases at the Hospital.

April 21, 1871. The continued encroachments by railroads upon the grounds of the Asylum had now resulted in completely encircling them with the iron tracks, and dividing them so as to make them unavailable and dangerous for the uses for which large portions of them had been purchased.

The Trustees were compelled to admit the almost proximate necessity of the removal of the institution to another site. The prospect of this necessity also prevented the Trustees from making any plans or large outlays for improvements, for new buildings, or even for repairs. On this date, the Trustees voted that Messrs. Eliot, Dalton, and Ellis be a Committee to make such inquiries as they deem expedient for a new site for the Asylum, and report to the Board.

June 30, 1871. On the recommendation of Dr. Shaw, it was voted, — "That the article and tables of statistics of surgical operations at the Hospital, recently prepared by Dr. Chadwick, be published in the 'Boston Medical and Surgical Journal,' with an edition of five hundred copies for distribution, at an expense not exceeding one hundred dollars."

December 31, 1871. The experiment of a separate ward for the treatment of patients afflicted with skin diseases, though by no means unsuccessful in its especial results, was regarded by the Trustees as open to some general objections, and was discontinued at the close of the year. Dr. James C. White had on his own part made a most faithful trial of the experiment, and had devoted to it his skill and experience in his specialty. He continues to serve the institution as Chemist and Physician to patients with diseases of the skin.

In closing his continuation of the History, Dr. Ellis remarks : —

"To the residents in this immediate community, the names of those who for so long a series of years have successively served as Trustees of this institution will make it unnecessary to add anything as to their claims to confidence and respect, for the services they have rendered. Considering what sort of men have been elected, and from what ranges of life they come, the wonder is that the Hospital bears on its records, often for a considerable series of years, the names which are found upon them. That gentlemen, most of whom might plead the engrossment of their own private affairs or business agencies, have been found from year to year to give their time and the indorsement of their reputation to these exacting tasks, is to be regarded simply as a tribute paid by them to the cause of humanity as represented by the Hospital."

"It is enough for us to have the assurance that, in both Hospital and Asylum, the highest appliances of science and the gentlest ministrations of a refined humanity are engaged for each human malady as if it were a case by itself."

OFFICERS OF THE HOSPITAL

FROM ITS FOUNDATION TO 1872.

PRESIDENTS.

WILLIAM PHILLIPS, from 1814 through 1826.
THOMAS H. PERKINS, from 1826 through 1827.
JOHN LOWELL, from 1828 to January, 1830.
GARDINER GREENE, from June, 1830, through 1832.
JOSEPH HEAD, from 1833 through 1835.
EBENEZER FRANCIS, during 1836.
EDWARD TUCKERMAN, from 1837 to 1843.
WILLIAM APPLETON, from 1844 to 1862.
ROBERT HOOPER, from 1862 to 1869.
EDWARD WIGGLESWORTH, 1869 to 1875.

VICE-PRESIDENTS.

SAMUEL PARKMAN, elected 1814 and declined serving.
JAMES PERKINS, from 1815 till death, in August, 1822.
THOMAS H. PERKINS, from 1823 to June, 1826.
JOHN LOWELL, from June, 1826, to June, 1829.
GARDINER GREENE, from June, 1829, to June, 1830.
JOSEPH HEAD, from June, 1830, through 1832.
EBENEZER FRANCIS, from 1833 through 1835.
SAMUEL APPLETON, during 1836.
JONATHAN PHILLIPS, from 1837 through 1845.
THEODORE LYMAN, from 1846 till death, in 1849.
ROBERT HOOPER, from 1850 to 1856.
NATHANIEL I. BOWDITCH, from 1856 to 1862.
EDWARD WIGGLESWORTH, from 1862 to 1869.
NATHANIEL THAYER, from 1869 to 1883.

TREASURERS.

JAMES PRINCE, from 1813 till death in February, 1821.
WILLIAM COCHRAN, from February 28, 1821, for 6 months till death.
N. P. RUSSELL, from September 14, 1821, through 1834.
HENRY ANDREWS, from 1835 to 1859.
J. THOMAS STEVENSON, from 1859 to August, 1875.

SECRETARIES.

RICHARD SULLIVAN, from 1811 through 1816.
HENRY CODMAN, from 1817 through 1826.
N. I. BOWDITCH, from 1827 to June, 1836.
WILLIAM GRAY, from June, 1836, through 1841.
MARCUS MORTON, jun., from 1842 to 1859.
THOMAS B. HALL, from 1859 to 1865.
WILLIAM S. DEXTER, for 1865.
THOMAS B. HALL, from 1866 to ——

TRUSTEES.

THOMAS H. PERKINS, from 1813 through 1818.
JOSIAH QUINCY, from 1813 through 1820.
DANIEL SARGENT, from 1813 through 1821.
JOSEPH MAY, from 1813 to November 5, 1826.
STEPHEN HIGGINSON, jun., from 1813 through 1815.
GAMALIEL BRADFORD, from 1813 through 1823.
TRISTRAM BARNARD, from 1813 through 1818.
GEORGE G. LEE, from 1813 through 1816.
FRANCIS C. LOWELL, from 1813 through 1815.
JOSEPH TILDEN, from 1813 through 1815.
JOHN L. SULLIVAN, from 1813 through 1816.
RICHARD SULLIVAN, from 1813 to 1822.
JONATHAN PHILLIPS, from 1816 to July, 1832.
JOHN LOWELL, from 1816 through 1819.
JOSEPH COOLIDGE, from 1816 through 1831.
DAVID SEARS, from 1817 through 1819.
EBEN FRANCIS, part of 1817; chosen by Corporation, 1818 (resigned for part of 1820), through 1831.

Peter C. Brooks, elected 1819 but declined serving.
Joseph Head, elected by Trustees in 1819; by Corporation, 1820, to June, 1829.
Thomas W. Ward, elected by Trustees in 1819; by Corporation, 1820, through 1823.
Samuel Appleton, elected by Trustees in October, 1819; by Corporation, 1820, to December, 1822.
John Belknap, from 1820, through 1822.
Daniel P. Parker, from 1821 to July 26, 1825.
Theodore Lyman, jun., from 1822 to July 26, 1825.
Benjamin Guild, from 1823 to January, 1834.
William H. Prescott, from 1823 to July 26, 1825.
Gardiner Greene, from 1823 to July, 1830.
Samuel Swett, from May, 1823, to July, 1826.
Edward Tuckerman, from 1824 through 1836.
George Ticknor, from July, 1826, to July, 1830.
Edward H. Robbins, from July, 1826, through 1834.
William Sturgis, from July, 1826, to July, 1827.
Amos Lawrence, from December 5, 1826, to February 26, 1831.
P. T. Jackson, from July, 1827, to July, 1828.
Henry Codman, from July, 1827, to January, 1835.
Wm. H. Gardiner, from July, 1828 [one year].
Francis C. Gray, from July, 1829, to October 30, 1836.
Josiah Quincy, jun., from July, 1830, through 1836.
Benj. D. Greene, from August 26, 1830, to October 8, 1833.
James Bowdoin, elected August, 1830, declined serving.
Heman Lincoln, elected January, 1831, declined serving.
George Bond, elected February, 1831, died May 23, 1842.
George Hallet, elected July, 1831, through 1833.
Thomas W. Ward, re-elected 1832 and declined serving.
Abbott Lawrence, from July, 1832, through 1835.
Francis J. Oliver, from 1833 through 1835.
Samuel A. Eliot, from 1834 through 1838.
Charles G. Loring, from 1834 through 1837.
Rufus Wyman, elected 1835 and declined serving.
Thomas B. Curtis, from 1835 through 1838.
Charles Amory, from 1836 through 1847.
Henry Edwards, from 1836 through 1845.
Samuel Lawrence, from 1836 through 1838.

ROBERT G. SHAW, from 1836 through 1838.
JOHN P. THORNDIKE, from 1836 through 1837.
MARTIN BRIMMER, from 1837 through 1842.
ROBERT HOOPER, jun., from 1837 through 1849.
N. I. BOWDITCH, from 1837 to 1856.
WILLIAM APPLETON, from 1838 through 1841.
THOMAS LAMB, from 1838 to 1861.
GEORGE M. DEXTER, from 1839 to 1853.
FRANCIS C. LOWELL, from 1839 to 1853.
HENRY B. ROGERS, (omitting 1840) from 1839 to 1874.
EBENEZER CHADWICK, from 1840 through 1842.
IGNATIUS SARGENT, [during] 1841.
WILLIAM T. ANDREWS, from 1842 through 1847.
JONATHAN CHAPMAN, [during] 1843.
WILLIAM F. OTIS, [during] 1843.
JOHN A. LOWELL, from 1843 through 1850.
CHARLES S. STORROW, from 1844 through 1845.
EDWARD WIGGLESWORTH, from 1844 to 1862.
WILLIAM W. STONE, [during] 1846.
J. WILEY EDMUNDS, from 1847 through 1848.
J. THOMAS STEVENSON, from 1846 to 1859.
CHARLES H. MILLS, from 1848 to 1859.
AMOS A. LAWRENCE, from 1848 to 1854.
WILLIAM S. BULLARD, from 1849 to 1872.
G. HOWLAND SHAW, from 1850 to 1856.
WILLIAM J. DALE, from 1851 to 1862, and for 1864.
JOHN P. BIGELOW, from 1852 to 1855, and for 1857.
CHARLES H. WARREN, from 1853 to 1857.
ROBERT M. MASON, from 1854 to 1862.
HENRY M. HOLBROOK, from 1855 to 1857.
JAMES B. BRADLEE, from 1856 to 1859.
WILLIAM D. GREENOUGH, from 1856 to 1866.
JOHN LOWELL, from 1857 to 1870.
ABBOTT LAWRENCE, from 1858 to 1859.
NATHANIEL H. EMMONS, from 1859 to 1861.
GEORGE HIGGINSON, from 1859 to 1872.
MARCUS MORTON, jun., from 1859 to 1860.
MARTIN BRIMMER, from 1860 to 1864.
JAMES M. BEEBE, from 1860 to 1875.

J. AMORY DAVIS, from 1861 to 1866.
SAMUEL G. HOWE, from 1861 to 1875.
JAMES C. WILD, from 1862 to 1865.
HARRISON RITCHIE, from 1863 to 1867.
HENRY A. WHITNEY, from 1863 to 1868.
CHARLES S. STORROW, from 1865 to 1870.
CHARLES H. DALTON, from 1866 to 1881.
SAMUEL ELIOT, from 1866 to 1898.
JAMES L. LITTLE, from 1866 to 1871.
EZRA FARNSWORTH, from 1867 to 1872.
EDMUND DWIGHT, from 1868 to ——.
GEORGE S. HALE, from 1870 to 1888.
SAMUEL W. SWETT, from 1870 to 1872.
GEORGE E. ELLIS, from 1871 to 1875.
SAMUEL D. WARREN, from 1871 to 1888.
HENRY P. KIDDER, from 1872 to 1886.

CHAIRMEN OF THE TRUSTEES.

THOMAS H. PERKINS, 1818.
JOSEPH MAY, 1819, to November, 1826.
JOSEPH HEAD, December 5, 1826, to July, 1829.
EBENEZER FRANCIS, July, 1829, to July, 1831.
EDWARD TUCKERMAN, July, 1831, to February, 1835.
GEORGE BOND, from February, 1835, to May, 1842.
ROBERT HOOPER, jun., June 19, 1842, to January, 1850.
N. I. BOWDITCH, 1850 to 1856.
HENRY B. ROGERS, from 1856 to 1874.

SUPERINTENDENTS OF HOSPITAL.

[OFFICE ABOLISHED IN 1858.]

Capt. NATHANIEL FLETCHER, April 21, 1821, died May 1, 1825.
NATHAN GURNEY, June 12, 1825, to November, 1833.
GAMALIEL BRADFORD, October 11, 1833, died October 23, 1839.
CHARLES SUMNER, December 17, 1839, to March 21, 1841.
JOHN M. GOODWIN, March 21, 1841, to November 2, 1845.
RICHARD GIRDLER, November 16, 1845, to 1858.

RESIDENT PHYSICIANS OF HOSPITAL.

BENJAMIN S. SHAW, from 1858 to 1872.
NORTON FOLSOM, elected May 3, 1872.

PHYSICIANS OF ASYLUM.

GEORGE PARKMAN, conditionally elected October 4, 1816, never served.
RUFUS WYMAN, March 23, 1818, to May 31, 1835.
THOMAS G. LEE, chosen January 16, 1835, died October, 1836.
LUTHER V. BELL, December 11, 1836, to 1856, and temporarily for 1857.
CHAUNCEY BOOTH, from 1856, died January 13, 1858.
JOHN E. TYLER, from 1858 to 1871.
GEORGE F. JELLY, elected October 13, 1871.

INDEX OF SUBJECTS.

Additions to Hospital. Proposed, 26. New wings, 37, 40. New kitchen, 39. Cost of, 41. Building for offensive diseases, 52, 53.

Apollo. Statue of, 37, 42.

Apothecary. Nomination of rejected, 15. At Hospital, to be styled the House Physician, 23. At Asylum, to be known as the Assistant Physician, 33. To be chosen annually, 34.

Appropriations. An extra grant of $500 for aid in regard to new buildings, 19. A grant of $100 for faithful services, 22. A grant of $1,000 for long, zealous and unwearied exertions, 27. For defraying expenses of last illness, and payment of five months' salary to widow, 28. A grant of $250 for increased and arduous duties, 29. A grant of six months' salary to the widow of an official, 32. A grant of eight months' salary to an official who had resigned, 37. $500 placed at disposal of Asylum Superintendent for the relief of poor patients, 39, 40. For expenses of Asylum Superintendent to a professional meeting, 39. $25 toward buying a wooden leg for a Hospital patient, 40. For the purchase of a wedding gift to two faithful employés, 41. For the expenses of a distinguished anatomist who died in the Hospital, 42. For the settlement of a claim for compensation for a cow, killed while boarded at the Asylum, 43. $25 in aid of a patient who has become blind, 44. For the presentation of a gold watch to a faithful official, 51. $1,000 to the fund for Dr. W. T. G. Morton, 55. A grant of three months' salary to an official who had resigned, 57. For payment of wages to Hospital nurse, who had been relieved of all duties, 60. For payment of salary of Matron for three months after her resignation, 60. For payment of two months' salaries to Asylum Steward and Matron, after their resignations, 64. For payment of salary of Superintendent of Asylum, during a year's leave of absence, 65. $100 for a gift to a kitchen attendant, 69. *Refused* for a monument to Dr. Morton, 70. $200 for pictures in the wards, 71.

Artist of the Hospital. Office of, established, 55, 56.

Asylum. Site for, at Somerville, 9. Ground plan for, 9. Not designed exclusively for the wealthy, 9. Proposed buildings, 10. First patient, 14. Library, 16, 58. Named for Mr. M'Lean, 20. Head of, to be known as Physician and Superintendent, 26. House Apothecary to be known as Assistant Physician, 33. Gift of $10,000, for the benefit of poor patients, 35. Engraving of, 37. Gift of $20,000, for the benefit of rich patients, 42. Alleged maltreatment of patient investigated, 46, 47. Admission of inebriates forbidden, 59. Criticisms of, by patients, 60, 61. A chapel proposed, 69. A Chaplain appointed, 69. Daily life of patients described, 28, 71. Necessity of new site for, 73, 74.

Bigelow Operating Chair, 51.

Box. For preservation of valuable papers, 35.

Chapel at Asylum. Plan for, 69.

Charter. Grant of, 6.

Chloroform. Causes death of a patient, 49.

Chemist and Microscopist. Office of, established, 46. Duties of Microscopist assigned to Curator of Pathological Cabinet, 53.

Children. To be received at Hospital, 70.

Circular Letters and Addresses. Inviting subscriptions for a hospital, 5, 8, 9, 36.

Coffee. Purchase of "domestic," forbidden, 22.

Colored Man. Admission to Hospital criticised, 24. Admission refused, 28, 29. Gift of twenty-five cents from, 36.

Committee on Alterations and Repairs. Establishment of, 59, 60.

Corporate Name. Decision against change of, 20.

Corporation. Charter, 6. First meeting, 7. Record book, 7. By-Laws adopted, 7, 15. Authorized to grant annuities on lives, 8. Common Seal adopted, 12. Date for Annual Meeting changed, 26. Trustees to be considered members of, 32. Not a "State Charity," 66.

Erysipelatous Inflammation. At Hospital, 21.

Ether Discovery, 39, 40. Reference to first capital operation by use of, 44.

Donation-book. Established, 22.

Fence at Hospital. 54, 55.

Free Beds in Hospital. Established, 15. Yearly price for, 19, 58. Price for life, 19, 28. Grant of, for life, 31. Perpetual free-bed established, 68. Tablets over, undesirable, 34, 40. Standing Committee on, 38.

General Hospital. Site for, 10. Defect in title, 11. Bulfinch plan adopted, 12. Corner stone laid, 13. Centre and East Wing finished, 14. Officers exempt from military duty, 15. First patient, 15. Free beds established, 15. West Wing finished, 16. Library, 16, 35, 40, 51. Salt-water bathing house erected, 18. Visited by General Lafayette, 19. Removal of patients from, on account of erysipelatous inflammation, 21. The Apothecary to be styled the House Physician, 23. Fire in East Wing, 23. Silver spoons bought, 23. Wedding of Superintendent, 24. Windows overlooking Hospital Garden, 26, 27, 32. Enlargement of building proposed, 26. Syphilitic patients to be received only in urgent cases, 32. Small-pox introduced, 33. Erection of two new wings authorized, 37. View from Trustees' room described, 38. New kitchen, etc., 39. New East Wing finished, 40. Cost of additions and repairs, 41. Gas introduced, 42. Mistake causes death of a patient, 49. Complete set of Hospital Reports, etc., 51. Building for patients with offensive diseases, 52, 53. Lecture and Reception Room converted into wards, 54. New fence around the grounds, 54, 55. Average time of the stay of patients, 51. Room for Treadwell Library, 57. Incurable cases not to be admitted, 59. Dental Service established, 69. Separate ward for skin diseases established, 73; discontinued, 74.

Gifts [of an extraordinary kind]. A mahogany medicine case, 14. Proceeds of the exhibition of a picture, 14. A patent for sweeping chimneys, 14. A model of a machine called a "gout-frame," 15. A bedstead and other articles, 15. $400, "to be repaid if the donor needs it," 16. A mummy from Thebes, 16, 17. A sow "of uncommonly fine breed," 18. Trees and shrubs for Hospital grounds, 21. Twenty shares of stock, not to be sold for ten years, without the consent of donor, 25. $1,000 for the purchase of religious and moral books, 33. $10,000 for the benefit of poor patients at Asylum, 35. Statue of Apollo, 37, 42. $100 invested in silver spoons for the Asylum, 37. A tomb, in trust, 38. $20,000 for the benefit of rich patients at Asylum, 42. $5,000 to constitute a " Wooden-leg Fund," 61. $2,000 as a fund for History of the Hospital, 61. Fund of $2,000 for prizes, 67. Portrait of M. Louis, of Paris, 68, 69. Surgical instruments, $3,250 in value, 72, 73. $1,250 for a Surgical Instrument Fund, 72, 73. Twenty-five cents, "from a poor black," 36.

"Gout-frame." Model of, 15.

Harvard College. Joins the Hospital in a suit *versus* the surviving Trustee under John M'Lean's will, 17, 18. Decline the Treadwell bequest, 57.

History of the Hospital, 46, 61.

Hospital Grounds. Bought, 10. Defect in title to, 10, 11, 12. Value of, 12. Trees and Shrubs for, 21. Windows overlooking, 26, 27, 32. Rain-gauge in, 35. New fence round, 40, 54, 55. Opportunity for improving, 53. Filling of adjoining flats, 58.

Hospital Patients. Average time of stay, 51.

Hospital Staff. Appointed, 10. Duties of, defined, 27.

House Physicians and Surgeons. Nomination of, 33.

House Pupils. Trustees' answer to an inquiry from, 47, 48. Permitted to sleep and breakfast at Hospital, 60. To board at Hospital, 61.

Inebriates. Admission of, to Asylum forbidden, 59.

Jews. Gifts from, 15, 18, 51, 52.

Letter. A *painted*, 26.

Library, 16, 35, 40, 56, 58.

Massachusetts Hospital Life Insurance Company. Hospital entitled to share of its profits, 8. Hospital subscribe for stock in, 16. Receipts of Hospital from, 60.

Massachusetts Medical Society. Meeting of, at Hospital, 69.

Medical College. Opinion of Trustees on erection of, in vicinity of Hospital, 38, 39.

Medical Library. Established at Hospital, 40.

Medical Students. Proposition to charge a fee for admission of, 65. Women refused admission as, 56, 57. Women granted admission as, 66.

Microscope. Purchase of, 40.

Microscopist and Curator of the Pathological Cabinet. Office of, established, 53. Allowed to perform duties of Visiting Physicians, 64.

Military Duty. Officers from Hospital exempt from, 15.

Mummy from Thebes. Gift of, 16, 17.

Officers of the Hospital. List of, 76, 77, 78, 79, 80, 81.

Pathological Museum. Established, 52, 53.

Physicians and Surgeons. First appointed, 10. Notified that Hospital will be ready for patients, 15. Receive General

Lafayette at Hospital, 19. Allowed to charge for extra services rendered to a Hospital patient, 24. Memorial from, as to a new building, 26. Duties of, defined, 27. Violation of rule by, 29, 30. To nominate House Physicians and Surgeons, 33. Urged to prevent spread of small-pox in Hospital, 33. Requested to suggest changes in Hospital, 35. May charge fees to out-door patients, 36. Recommend appointment of a Chemist and Microscopist, 46. Establishment of a Pathological Museum, 52, 53. Communication from, with reference to House Pupils, 47, 48. To direct Artist of the Hospital, 56. Request a change in the regulations, 64. Conference with, 21, 72. Resignation of, 30, 31, 32, 44, 50, 54, 63, 71. Death of, 66, 67.

Physician to Out-patients. Office of, established, 57. May charge fees, 36, 64.

Portraits. Loan of, refused, 23. Loaned, 21, 64. Tablets placed under, 47, 51. Hon. William Phillips, painting by Stuart, 16, 21. John M'Lean, painting by Stuart, 17, 18. Samuel Eliot, painting by Stuart, 17, 20. Thomas Oliver, painting, 18, 27, 28. Abraham Touro, painting, 18. Jeremiah Belknap, painting by Sargent, 25, 26. Dr. James Jackson, bust by S. V. Clevenger, 1839, 31, 34. Daniel Waldo, painting, 37, 38. Israel Munson, painting, 37, 38. Dr. John C. Warren, bust by Richard Greenough, 50, 51. Dr. Jacob Bigelow, bust by Henry Dexter, 54. Dr. Luther V. Bell, painting, 55. Dr. George Hayward, bust by Henry Dexter, 1857, 55. Dr. M. S. Perry, photograph, 59. Nathaniel I. Bowditch, photograph, 61. William Appleton, bust by Henry Dexter, 63. Dr. Solomon D. Townsend, bust by T. Ball, 1864, 63. M. Louis (of Paris), painting, 68, 69.

Post-Mortem Register. Established, 72.

Province-house Estate. Grant of, 6. Leased for ninety-nine years, 6. Application to buy reversionary interest in, 22.

Publication. Of results obtained by Chemist and Microscopist, 46. Of yearly medical and surgical cases, 73. Of statistics of surgical operations, 74.

Records. Of Corporation, 7. Of Trustees, 7. Of Donations, 22, 35, 36. Of Medical and Surgical cases, 32, 33. Of Devises and bequests, 35, 44. Post-mortem, 72.

Religious Services. At Hospital, 19, 70. At Asylum, 28, 29, 34, 51, 59, 66, 69 [a chapel proposed], 70, 71.

Resident Physician. Office of, established, 57. Leave of absence granted to, for government service, 63. Allowed to accept government office, 63.

Reward. Offered for a plan of a Hospital, 12.

Rules and Regulations. For the asylum revised, 23. New draft of, for Hospital and Asylum, 24. Violation of, at Hospital censured, 29. Amendments of, 33, 55, 56, 58, 59, 60, 64, 65, 66, 72.

Secretary. Granted a salary, 9. Directed to audit accounts, 22. Instructed to record all devises and bequests in a special book, 44.

Skin Diseases. Separate ward for, established, 73; discontinued, 74.

Small Pox. At Hospital, 33.

State Prison. Work of convicts on stone for Hospital, 10.

Subscriptions. For building Hospital, 9, 10, 36. For Hospital fence, 55. List of, 35.

Surgeon to Out-patients. Office of, established, 64. May charge fees, 64.

Syphilitic Patients. Excluded from Hospital, 32.

Tin Case. Used for holding the title-deeds, 9, 22.

Tobacco. Use of, prohibited, 34, 36, 41.

Treadwell Library, 56, 57.

Treasurer. Invited to attend meetings of Trustees, 9; and to participate in their discussions, 59. Salary of, 38, 69. Reports income of 7.70 per cent on investments, 73.

Trustees. Mentioned in charter, 6. First chosen, 7. First Record book, 7. First meeting, 8. Meetings held at Athenæum, 9. Approve act of committee which exceeded their powers, 9. Arrange Visiting Committees, 13, 15, 24. Discontinue meetings on Sunday, 15. Refuse to confirm a nomination, 15. Demand a quarterly analysis of the accounts, 19. Accept actual possession of a bequest, agreeing to pay an annuity thereon, 19. Receive General Lafayette at Hospital, 19. Forbid purchase of " domestic coffee," 22. Authorize purchase of carriage and horses for use of Asylum patients, 22. Decline to loan portraits by Stuart, 23. Consider intended marriage of Hospital Superintendent, 24. Retire from office on account of absence in Europe, 26, 43, 61. Define duties of Hospital Staff, 27. Present an annual report of six lines, 28. Authorize purchase of piano-forte and billiard tables for the asylum, 28, 31. All absent from a meeting, 28, 42, 44. Censure a violation of the Rules and Regulations, 29, 30. Accept one-quarter part of a bequest, on proposal of heirs-at-law for a compromise, 31, 32. To be considered members of the Corporation, 32. Direct House Physician and Surgeon to record all cases, 33. Permit erection of pole for rain-gauge in Hospital grounds, 35. Appoint Standing Committee on Free Beds, 38. Authorize erection of monument to memory of deceased donors, 39. A practising physician appointed a Trustee, 43. Investigate alleged maltreatment of a patient at Asylum, 46, 47. Assert their supreme power in Hospital affairs, 47, 48. Change the day and the place for their meetings, 49. Investigate the death of a patient caused by the mistake of the Hospital Apothecary, 49. Establish a Pathological Museum at the Hospital, 53. Establish the office of Artist of the Hospital, 55, 56. Refuse to admit women as students at the Hospital, 56, 57, 63. Establish the office of Resident Physician, 57. Surrender their legal rights to an estate, 58. Invite the Treasurer to participate in their discussions, 59. Appoint Standing Committee on Alterations and Repairs, 59, 60. Permit House Pupils to sleep and breakfast at Hospital, 60; to board at Hospital, 61. Choose temporary Chairman, 60, 62. Assure the Governor of their desire to care for diseased or wounded soldiers, and prepare to do so, 61, 62; but decline to contract for such service, 62. Grant Resident Physician and Superintendent of Asylum leaves of absence for government service, 63. Allow Resident Physician to accept a government office, 63. Appoint a Committee to watch State legislation, 63. Allow Dr. Bell's portrait to be temporarily removed from Asylum, 64. Establish office of Surgeon to Out-patients, 64. Authorize Physicians and Surgeons to Out-patients to charge fees, 64. Vote to hold regular meetings on Friday instead of Sunday, 64. Admit female students to the Hospital, 66. Appoint women as visitors to the Hospital, 70.

Visiting Committee. Arranged, 13, 15. Dismiss patient, 18. To visit unattended by officials, 19. Report on rates of board, 21. Appointed to revise rules and regulations for Asylum, 23. Important change in arrangement of, 24, 25. Authorized "to procure a water-bed," 33. To sign entries in "Post-mortem Register," 72.

Wards. Report on naming, 44.

Warren Fund. Established, 33. Annual Committee for purchase of books under, 37.

Warren Prize Fund. Established, 67.

Water Rates. Reduction of, refused, 64.

Wedding. At Hospital, 24.

Windows. Overlooking Hospital Garden, 26, 27, 32.

Women. Admission of, as medical students refused, 56, 57, 63; granted, 66. Appointed visitors, 70, 71.

Wooden-leg Fund. Diversion of income from specified purpose objected to, 64.

INDEX OF NAMES.

Abbott, Dr. Samuel L., 57.
Amory, Charles, 36, 40, 43, 78.
Andrew, Governor, 61.
Andrews, Henry, 77.
Andrews, William T., 35, 36, 37, 39, 42, 79.
Appleton, Samuel, 76, 78.
Appleton, William, 35, 42, 43, 63, 76, 79.

Bacon, Dr. John, jun., 53.
Barnard, Tristram, 77.
Beebe, James M., 66, 69, 79.
Belknap, Jeremiah, 25, 26, 39.
Belknap, John, 78.
Belknap, Mary, 25, 39.
Bell, Dr. Luther V., 29, 34, 35, 37, 39, 46, 54, 55, 64, 81.
Bigelow, Dr. Henry J., 51, 65, 72, 73.
Bigelow, Dr. Jacob, 54.
Bigelow, John P., 79.
Blake, Sophia, 66.
Blanchard, Hezekiah, 11.
Bond, George, 32, 42, 78, 80.
Booth, Dr. Chauncey, 37, 81.
Bowditch, Mary I., 71.
Bowditch, Nathaniel I., 30, 31, 32, 34, 35, 37, 40, 42, 46, 51, 61, 64, 76, 77, 79, 80.
Bowditch, Dr. Henry I., 40, 59.

Bowdoin, James, 6, 78.
Boylston, Thomas, 5.
Bradford, Dr. Gamaliel, 32, 77, 80.
Bradford, Mrs. Dr. Gamaliel, 32.
Bradlee, James B., 79.
Brimmer, Martin, 32, 34, 79 (lines 3 and 38).
Brooks, Peter C., 78.
Bryant, Eliza, 27.
Bulfinch, Charles, 9, 10, 12.
Bullard, William S., 52, 62, 63, 65, 66, 72, 79.
Bunker, Mrs., 71.

Chadwick, Ebenezer, 79.
Chadwick, Dr. James Read, 74.
Chapman, Jonathan, 79.
Clancey, James, 49.
Clough, Sarah, 41.
Cobb, General, 24.
Cochran, William, 77.
Codman, Henry, 77, 78.
Colburn, James S., 10.
Coolidge, Joseph, 77.
Courtis, Ambrose S., 31.
Cüntz, Mrs. Otto, 71.
Curtis, Thomas B., 78.

Dale, Dr. William J., 43, 46, 62, 79.
Dalton, Charles H., 39, 72, 73, 74, 80.
Davis, J. Amory, 80.
Dexter, George M., 34, 36, 37, 39, 40, 42, 51, 79.
Dexter, William S., 77.
Dimmock, Susan, 66.
Dwight, Edmund, 80.

Edes, Robert B., 16.
Edmunds, J. Wiley, 79.
Edwards, Henry, 36, 78.
Eliot, Samuel, 17, 20, 66, 74, 80.
Eliot, Samuel A., 27, 28, 29, 31, 78.
Ellis, Dr. Calvin, 53, 64.
Ellis, The Rev. George E., 46, 74, 80.
Emmons, Nathaniel H., 79.
Everett, Hon. Edward, 37, 42.

Farnsworth, Ezra, 80.
Ferris, John, 41.
Fletcher, Capt. Nathaniel, 80.
Folsom, Dr. Norton, 81.
Fox, Dr., 37.
Francis, Ebenezer, 11, 14, 17, 19, 22, 23, 25, 26, 76, 77, 80.
Freeman, The Rev. Dr. James, 21.

Gallison, Sarah L., 60.
Gardiner, William H., 78.
Girdler, Capt. Richard, 57, 80.
Girdler, Mrs. Richard, 41.
Goodhue, Homer, 51.
Goodwin, John M., 37, 38, 80.
Gorham, Benjamin, 12.
Gray, Benjamin, 11, 12.
Gray, Francis C., 24, 28, 78.
Gray, William, 77.
Green, Dr., 15.
Greene, Benjamin D., 26, 43, 78.
Greene, Gardiner, 76, 78.
Greenough, David, 6, 22.
Greenough, William D., 79

Guild, Benjamin, 16, 17, 25, 78.
Gurney, Nathan, 22, 24, 80.
Gurney, Mrs. Nathan, 22, 24.

Hadley, Mr., 71.
Hale, Dr. Enoch, 35.
Hale, George S., 80.
Hall, Thomas B., 77.
Hall, William, 14.
Hallet, George, 78.
Harney, Madame, 71.
Haskins, The Rev. David G., 69, 71.
Hayward, Dr. George, 44, 55.
Head, Joseph, 25, 26, 76, 78, 80.
Hickford, Thomas W., 41.
Higginson, George, 79.
Higginson, Stephen, jun., 77.
Holbrook, Henry M., 79.
Hooper, Robert, 76.
Hooper, Robert, jun., 42, 79, 80.
Howe, Dr. Samuel G., 62, 63, 80.
Hunnewell, Hon. Jonathan, 21.

Jackson, F. H., 68.
Jackson, Dr. James, 5, 15, 30, 31, 34, 50, 67, 69.
Jackson, P. T., 78.
Jelly, Dr. George F., 81.
Joy, Benjamin, 9.

Kerr, Ann, 40.
Kidder, Henry P., 80.
Kilborn, Susan L., 63.

Lafayette, General, 19.
Lamb, Thomas, 31, 37, 56, 79.

Lambert, Mr., 16.
Lane, Frazier and Company, 5.
Lane, William H., 14.
Lawrence, Abbott, 78, 79.
Lawrence, Amos, 22, 25, 28, 29, 78.
Lawrence, Amos A., 46, 79.
Lawrence, Samuel, 78.
Lee, Francis, 25.
Lee, George G., 77.
Lee, Thomas, 25.
Lee, Dr. Thomas G., 28, 29, 81.
Loring, Charles G., 11, 66, 78.
Loring, Josiah, 7.
Louis, M., 68, 69.
Lowell, John, 11, 12, 55, 63, 76, 77, 79.
Lowell, John A., 43, 79.
Lowell, Francis C., 51, 77, 79.
Lincoln, Heman, 78.
Little, James L., 80.
Lyman, Theodore, 76.
Lyman, Theodore, jun., 16, 78.

Mason, Robert M., 56, 61, 79.
May, Colonel Joseph, 12, 13, 22, 77, 80.
Mills, Charles H., 79.
M'Intire, Elizabeth, 41.
M'Lean, John, 17, 18, 19, 20, 45.
M'Lean, Ann, 19, 20.
Moorhouse, Mr., 71.
Morton, Marcus, jun., 77, 79.
Morton, Dr. W. T. G., 39, 40, 55, 70.
Munson, Israel, 37.

Oberhausser, 40.
Oliver, Francis J., 78.

Oliver, Thomas, 18, 19, 27, 38.
Otis, Dr. George W., 23, 24.
Otis, William F., 79.

Parker, Daniel P., 78.
Parkman, George, 81.
Parkman, Samuel, 76.
Parsons, Gorham, 18.
Perkins, The Rev. Frederick T., 34.
Perkins, Helen A., 71.
Perkins, James, 13, 76.
Perkins, Colonel Thomas H., 8, 13, 76, 77, 80.
Perry, Dr. M. S., 59.
Phillips, Jonathan, 76, 77.
Phillips, Hon. William, 5, 10, 13, 16, 17, 21, 76.
Pinkerton, J. M., 64.
Prescott, Mrs., 27.
Prescott, Wiliam H., 78.
Prince, James, 77.
Prince, heirs, 10.
Putnam, Annie, 71.

Quincy, Josiah, 8, 11, 28, 29, 77.
Quincy, Josiah, jun., 78.

Raymond, Lydia N., 58.
Redman, John, 40.
Revere, Joseph W., 41.
Ritchie, Harrison, 80.
Robbins, Dr. Edward H., 21, 23, 24, 43, 78.
Roberts, Richard S., 26.
Rogers, Henry B., 35, 36, 40, 46, 52, 55, 56, 59, 60, 61, 62, 64, 65, 72, 79, 80.

Russell, N. P., 77.
Russell, William, 37.

Salisbury, Sarah W., 56, 57.
Sargent, Daniel, 77.
Sargent, Henry, 25.
Sargent, Ignatius, 79.
Sarti, Signor Antonio, 42.
Sarti, Madame, 42.
Sawyer, Matthias P., 58.
Sears, David, 13, 77.
Shaw, Dr. Benjamin Shurtleff, 57, 62, 63, 70, 73, 74, 81.
Shaw, G. Howland, 55, 79.
Shaw, Robert G., 32, 79.
Stevenson, J. Thomas, 46, 55, 77, 79.
Stone, William W., 79.
Storrow, Charles S., 65, 79, 80.
Stuart, Gilbert Charles, 16, 17, 18, 20, 23.
Sturgis, William, 78.
Sullivan, John L., 8, 77.
Sullivan, Richard, 77 (lines 8 and 28).
Sumner, Charles, 80.
Swett, Samuel, 78.
Swett, Samuel W., 80.

Tappan, Mr., 28.
Taylor, Rebecca, 60.
Thayer, Nathaniel, 65, 76.
Thorndike, John P., 79.
Ticknor, George, 24, 78.
Tilden, Bryant P., 16.
Tilden, Joseph, 77.
Touro, Abraham, 15, 18, 52.
Touro, Judah, 51, 52.

Townsend, Henrietta, 71.
Townsend, Dr. Solomon D., 63.
Treadwell, Dr. John G., 56, 57.
Trumbull, Joseph, 15.
Tuckerman, Edward, 42, 76, 78, 80.
Tyler, C., 64.
Tyler, Mr. and Mrs. Columbus, 29, 35, 64.
Tyler, Dr. John E., 59, 60, 63, 65, 70, 81.

Van Lennep, Jacob, 16.

Waldo, Daniel, 37.
Ward, Thomas W., 78 (lines 4 and 30).
Warren, Charles H., 79.
Warren, Dr. John C., 5, 15, 30, 32, 33, 38, 50, 67.
Warren, Dr. J. Mason, 30, 66.
Warren, Dr. J. Collins, 66.
Warren, Samuel D., 80.
Welles, Hon. John, 21.
Wells, family, 11.
White, Dr. James C., 71, 73, 74.
Whitney, Henry A., 80.
Wiggin, Benjamin, 14.
Wigglesworth, Edward, 35, 52, 60, 76, 79.
Wild, James C., 80.
Wilder, Dr. Charles W., 43.
Williams, John, 23.
Wyman, Dr. Rufus, 19, 22, 25, 26, 27, 78, 81.

Young, Caroline, 71.

www.ingramcontent.com/pod-product-compliance
Lightning Source LLC
Chambersburg PA
CBHW020901160426
43192CB00007B/1031